D0868760

Praise for *The Stone Carrier*

"Bob Ward's *The Stone Carrier* is both a smart thriller and an (appropriately) jittery look back at the literary bar scene of New York in the late 70s and early 80s, when the only high more potent than cocaine was the high of acclaim. Suffused with a blend of paranoia and nostalgia, Ward captures that world beautifully."

—Richard Price, bestselling author
and screenwriter

"With *The Stone Carrier* Robert Ward has whipped up a suspenseful tale that manages to be both witty and blood-soaked. We are in NYC during the 1970s, nights spent among hotshot literary figures and amiable starlets, everybody zonked on cocaine and ambition, then the guys with guns start mixing in, looking for a stash thief, and things fly loose. A helluva fine read."

—Daniel Woodrell, author of *Winter's Bone*

"Robert Ward's new book *The Stone Carrier* confirms his place among the first rank of mystery writers and the novel is wonderfully entertaining. He is the true artist of the genre, essential reading."

—Ken Bruen, author of
the Jack Taylor crime novels

"With *The Stone Carrier*, Robert Ward has written a kind of noir love letter to the drug-fueled and celebrity-drenched New York City of the 1970s. Think Tarantino remaking Scorsese's *Mean Streets* and you'll get the picture."

—Tim O'Mara, editor of *Down to the River*

"All the glitter and grit of 1970s' New York with a heaping dose of drugs, murder, and divided loyalties, but with the underlying thrills of a man struggling to clear his name. A fast and taut trip through trouble and toward redemption."

—Jeffery Hess, author of *No Salvation*

"This book does a stellar job of interspersing layered, character-rich scenes with ones of tension and, ultimately, action. The action itself is realistic, and therefore impactful. The way that Ward handles the ending is brilliantly tied to the subtext of fame, power, and greed (but mostly fame) and not only differs from the expected route in fitting fashion but is also thematically satisfying. Reads like it was written by an insider, and I was transported into his world!"

—Frank Zafiro, author of
the River City crime novels

THE STONE CARRIER

ALSO BY ROBERT WARD

Novels

Shedding Skin
Cattle Annie and Little Britches
The Sandman
Red Baker
The King of Cards
The Cactus Garden
Grace
Four Kinds of Rain

Featuring Agent Jack Harper

Total Immunity
The Best Bad Dream

Non-Fiction

Renegades:
My Wild Trip from Professor to New Journalist

ROBERT WARD

THE STONE CARRIER

Copyright © 2020 by Robert Ward

All rights reserved. No part of the book may be reproduced in any form or by any electronic or mechanical means, including information storage and retrieval systems, without permission in writing from the publisher, except by a reviewer who may quote brief passages in a review.

Down & Out Books
3959 Van Dyke Road, Suite 265
Lutz, FL 33558
DownAndOutBooks.com

The characters and events in this book are fictitious. Any similarity to real persons, living or dead, is coincidental and not intended by the author.

Cover design by Zach McCain

ISBN: 1-64396-052-0
ISBN-13: 978-1-64396-052-4

For Celeste and Robbie.

And to My Dear Friend and Brother Richard Price.

CHAPTER ONE

1978

After a night of boozing and snorting cocaine in Elaine's bathroom with his buddy Thaddeus Bryant, Joey Gardello should have gone home, taken a Placidyl and been fast asleep. Instead, he stood at his thinking spot underneath Glen Span Arch in Central Park, waiting for his brother Ray. Ray had left a message with his answering service, saying: "Meet me under the Arch at two a.m. Very important." Joey cursed the wind whipping through the trees and took deep breaths to chill out. What the hell could Ray want? Probably nothing at all. His brother worried a lot about Joey's lifestyle, his dope selling, the kind of people selling drugs put him in touch with. He was always trying to get him to get back to filmmaking. Like that was easy. Joey hadn't had a directing job for three years. His last little movie, *Stab*, had gotten good reviews from the horror crowd but had barely made it into the theaters. And it hadn't sold to television at all. So what was he going to do? Make fucking commercials? Yeah, that was fine...if you could get them. But it was a tough game. You had to know the right people.

What the fuck DID Ray want anyway? Well, whatever

it was, one thing Joey knew for sure, Ray was his brother, a big goof who had looked out for him when he was a kid. A serious worrywart, but Joey could count on him. He was the one person in the world that Joey absolutely trusted.

Maybe that was a little sad.

But one person was enough.

He shook his head, lit a Lucky, and walked back and forth. He and Ray had been coming to this spot since they were kids. Used to sit down with his back up against the bridge wall and just dream away the time. He knew it was a little weird. Most people liked to read or just daydream down by the pond, but he always liked it under here. It was cool on hot days and he could pretend he was in some kind of castle. Wow, the fantasies he used to have...sitting here with his comics and his 8-millimeter camera. And when weird people came by he'd film them like he was some great documentary filmmaker.

He made little movies all over the park, but this was his resting spot, sort of like his editing room. Where he could gather his thoughts.

Which he had to do now. There was so much stuff going down. He really shouldn't spend all his time up at Elaine's with Thaddeus. Snorting coke in the bathroom with Hunter Thompson. And who else was that in there tonight? Oh yeah, Richard Harris. *A Man Called Horse* himself. Yeah, it was a blast, but he couldn't play around anymore.

Things had gotten serious in a hurry and he had to get his shit together. It was hard, though. He had never had enough discipline. He knew it. But, then again, discipline was overrated, right? He had the talent, tons of it. And a plan. Yeah, one hell of a plan.

His stock was headed up, with a bullet.

He took another deep breath. He could feel the coke wearing off, leaving that horrible medicinal taste in his mouth. He'd have to quit hitting that stuff too.

And he would. He was still young. He had time on his side, baby, just like The Rolling Stones.

It was going to be all right.

A few more minutes and he'd talk to Ray, then go back home, sleep it off. Tomorrow, new man.

He remembered Thaddeus, Ray and himself out in the streets as kids. Playing gangsters and G-Men. Pointing imaginary machine guns at one another. "Rattatat. Gotcha." "No, you didn't. I ducked the shots." "Nah, you are dead." "Okay, I am, but now I get up and I'm a New Man."

Yeah, that's how it was when you were a kid. You never worried about getting old, being broke or dying. It was like you were an actor in a movie.

Of course, real life wasn't like that.

But there was such a thing as being reborn while you were alive. Yeah, and that was just where he was now. On the verge of being reborn.

The wind whipped through him. Okay, the drugs were wearing off and now he was tired as hell. And where was...wait. Right there, walking up the dark path. A big guy with a shambling walk.

He wanted to be pissed at Ray for dragging him out here, but he couldn't. Nah. His bro was a great guy...

"Hey, you maniac," Joey said in greeting.

"Hey, you maniac yourself," Big Ray said.

They hugged one another, and nearly talked in unison: "So what the hell do you want? Dragging me out here in the middle of..."

They both stopped.

3

"I got a message from you on my service," Joey said. "Saying to meet you here at two a.m."

"But I got the same message from you on MY service."

"You didn't send me any message?" Joey said.

Ray shook his head.

"No way. What do you think is going on?"

Joey felt cold in his arms, and his mouth was suddenly dry.

"I don't know what it is, but I do know that we need to get the fuck out of here right now."

Ray looked around wildly but could see nothing through the dense trees and brush.

"Jesus, we being set up? What did you do, Joey? Did you steal coke from Nicky Baines? Did you?"

Joey looked too panicked to answer. Which way should they go—through the tunnel, back the way they came toward the West side, or farther into the park? Thinking furiously, he decided to go deeper into the park. If someone was setting them up, they'd assume they'd run for the nearest exit to the street, where they'd be safer.

"Come on, bro," Joey said, pulling Ray behind him and heading into the trees ahead.

"But, man, we should go for the street," Ray said. He wasn't moving at all. Terrified, he simply stood stock still.

"Goddamn it, Ray, listen to me. C'mon."

He yanked at his brother's arm, like a father pulling a stubborn kid.

Finally, Ray shuffled along behind him.

They got to the lip of the tunnel and peered out. No one there or at least no one they could see.

Joey whispered to his brother.

"When we come out of the tunnel we'll be in the open

4

on the path. So don't stay on it. Cut right into the bushes to the right, and I'll go left."

"No way," Ray said. "We gotta stick together."

"Uh-uh. Together we're easier targets."

"Shit."

"Okay, one, two, three, go!"

They stepped out of the tunnel, but before they could move either way, Ray was shot dead in his tracks. Two bullets hit him in the middle of his body, piercing his heart.

Joey couldn't help himself. He knelt down to see if he could help his brother.

And was himself shot twice, in the chest. For a second it was like they were kids again, wrestling around on the floor.

Joey looked up. Maybe he could see who the shooter was. But all he could see was the half moon, hanging over him like a cheap prop.

When his head fell on his brother's chest, he saw a piece of trash blowing toward him, one of those paper cups with the blue Parthenon painted on it.

Funny thing, he'd always wanted to make a movie in Greece.

Then he heard a long sigh, his own life leaking out of him. He lay his confused head on Big Ray's body and died.

CHAPTER TWO

Three Hours Earlier

The trick, Terry Brennan thought, was not to turn around and STARE! This was simply not done. Of course, it was okay to sort of twist your neck around and look every once in a while. The thing you couldn't do was actually turn all the way around and gawk. Definitely not allowed. Gawking was for the losers, the Bridge and Tunnel Crowd at the bar. They stood there in their lime-colored shirts and their reindeer print sleeveless sweaters which they bought at J.C. Penney's out at the Paramus Mall in freaking New Jersey and they drank their overpriced drinks and their heads swiveled back and forth as the famous and the infamous came through the front door and were seated at the tables along the side wall and in the back of the front room. Terry knew a couple of them by name, Jerry, from Queens who came with autograph book in hand; Dot, a secretary from mid-town; and most of all Big C, Clarence, something or other, from Caldwell, New Jersey. Clarence seemed the most desperate to Terry. Occasionally, he would get antsy and would rush up to Gianni, the maître d', and demand to be seated "back there" next to Woody Allen and Mariel Hemingway. And Gianni, all smiles and charm, would say, "Sorry, sir, we have no tables right now, sir. But something may open up after a while. Meanwhile, why don't you have a drink at the front bar? You can see everything from there and I'll let you know." And poor Clarence would smile a sad grin and sometimes even slip Gianni a twenty, as if it that was going to do any good. Of course, Gianni would take the bill anyway, slip it into his pocket, then hustle back to the people sitting at the tables.

The poor sap, Terry thought. Yet, he didn't feel all that secure himself. It was nearly impossible for him to believe that he could really be in the same room with famous actors like Richard Harris, who was sitting across the table from the mind-bogglingly beautiful actress, Julie Christie. Divine Julie whom Terry had fallen in love with in her very first picture, *Billy Liar*. He remembered her running across the barren working-class street, a vision of perfection as she came closer and closer into view. So close that her stunning, fresh, and ridiculously sensual face took up the entire screen. Right then and there eighteen-year-old Terry, watching in the Playhouse Theater in his own working-class hometown of Baltimore, fell madly, irrevocably, and hopelessly in love with her. And now, here he was sitting ten feet away from her, looking at her, with his mouth hanging open. But only for a second. Shut that mouth up, son, or be known as a rube, a loser.

Terry took a quick hit of his vodka martini and temporarily wiped out all desire for the fabulous actress. Time to simply take in the glorious moment. Let's see, who else was there tonight?

Not just actors and show biz people. There were also political figures, writers, artists. There, in the very back corner was...Henry Freaking Kissinger dining with his wife Nancy. And right next to them there, at the next table, was writing heavyweight Norman Mailer, with his pal Jose Torres, the ex-light heavyweight champion boxer. And just a couple of tables over was Janice Dickinson, the world's most famous model, laughing her sly, sensual laugh with some balding, bloated Hamptons billionaire in his blue blazer and green pants with whales on them. A whale wearing his whales. Perfect. Of course, Janice and Whale Man were drinking Elaine's expensive champagne by the truckloads.

Yes, these, Terry thought, were the people who counted in New York. The ones who were written about in Page Six of the *New York Post* and in *New York Magazine*, the ones who were talked about at every media party. "Oh, I just saw Truman over at Elaine's. He didn't look well at all. He was practically falling off of Princess Lee's arm! And I hear his new book is going to be just scandalous."

They were the ones everyone wanted to know, to talk to, to hang with. Hell, these were the stars, the elite everyone else wanted to BE.

And now here he was. Terry freaking Brennan. At table two. Only two and a half years ago he was an assistant professor at this frozen upstate college, Hobart and William Smith, in godforsaken Geneva, New York, the place where drunken, burned out Dick Diver goes to die in Tender is The Night. And now, in a remarkable reinvention that even he could barely believe, he was Terry Brennan, ace journalist, for *Rolling Stone*, *GQ*, the *Village Voice* and *Sport*, sitting at one of the hallowed tables, being gawked at by the Bridge and Tunnellers. Here he was beside his best friend, one of the hottest novelists in the world,

Thaddeus Bryant, author of *The Debt*, a book that was not only a number one *New York Times* bestseller but a literary success as well. A novel which was, right this moment, being made into a monstro-big-budget drama, starring Dustin Hoffman, Roy Scheider and Genevieve Bujold. The premiere was only three weeks away, and Terry could scarcely believe that he was going to be attending it with Thaddeus.

When he thought of the way he'd lived only a couple of years ago, in that dismal upstate town with not one decent restaurant and no one to talk to except students and one or two sympathetic souls on the faculty, it blew his mind. Talk about the fast track.

Now, he sat there listening as Elaine Kauffman, the world's most famous saloon keeper, chatted with (really REALLY too hard to believe) Mick Jagger, at the very next table, Mick sitting there with three gorgeous models, all of them slobbering over him, saying, "Oh, Mick…Mick, you are so funny!", "Oh, Mick, we love your scarf!", "Oh God, Mick, *Beggars Banquet* is still my favorite album of all time!" Terry smiled to himself. He was three feet away from Mick Jagger. It was all he could do to keep from turning around and telling Mick what a huge Stones fan he was! But no. Not cool. Not cool at all. He had to consciously remind himself what Thaddeus had told him just the other night. "Of course you're excited about being here with the big boys, but remember, it just means that now you're a big boy yourself. Treat them like equals, Terry, not like you're some beseeching fan. It's great to be one of the stars. It's what everyone wants and you're there. So act like you belong!"

"Yeah, right," Terry said. "I get it. And I will!"

But, of course, he didn't get it. Not quite. Mick Jagger

was known all over planet earth and in the outer constellations, and Terry Brennan was known by maybe seven top editors and a few thousand magazine readers. But he also understood what Thaddeus was telling him. By being here, and getting mentioned in Page Six of *The Post*, he could tell the world that he was a player in the Big Game. And, once he became known, maybe that little extra juice would earn him a bigger advance on his own first novel, *Bad Boy*! And if *Bad Boy* was a hit, maybe he would become truly famous. Not as famous as Mick but maybe as famous as Thaddeus. Christ, maybe they would even make a big Hollywood movie out of his book. Why not?

He looked across the table at Elaine. Generous of body, with a cockeyed but warm smile, in New York she was as big a legend as any of her famous guests. From a humble artist's bar in the Village she'd built the number one celebrity hangout in New York. The celebs loved and feared her. If she decided, she didn't like you she could keep you from getting your table no matter how big you were.

Terry sighed and drank his whiskey. Okay, so he wasn't there yet, but at least he was farther along than Thaddeus's old pal, Joey Gardello. Joey the wannabe filmmaker, who had graduated from the New York University film school a few years back and still hadn't made anything but a few industrial flicks and one really bad horror film. His work barely paid half the rent on his pad on 77th Street and West End. The rest of his money came from dealing primo cocaine which all the celebs copped from him both here and down in the Village. In fact, Joey had used Terry's West Village pad a couple of times to deal to the guys who hung out at the famous Village writers' bar, The Lion's Head. Truth was, Terry felt a little weird about that.

Though he acted like he was cool with it all, hanging out with a coke dealer bothered him. He kind of wished he hadn't been so accommodating to Joey. But what the hell? He was here in New York. Everyone who was hip did coke, and no one had died from it yet, as far as he knew.

Still, there were some nights when he snorted the stuff and his heart started knocking in his chest so hard he couldn't catch his breath. That was seriously no fun. He had decided he'd use it but be moderate about it, not get hung up on it.

Terry smiled warmly at Elaine. Though she was pushing fifty she still hopped from table to table laughing and telling stories, as well as listening in on the priceless tales of her famous guests. Terry watched her put her liver-spotted hand over Thaddeus' and give him her lopsided smile.

"*The Debt* was so terrific," she said. "I stayed up until dawn reading it and I rarely do that anymore, baby. I can't wait until the movie. They still planning to screen it at the Ziegfeld?"

"Yes, they are. It's all shot and postproduction is done. In three weeks, we'll all be at the premiere." Thaddeus said, kissing her on the cheek. "You know I couldn't have written it without you."

"Oh God, cut it out," Elaine said. "Don't bullshit a bullshitter."

She laughed and looked across the table at Terry.

"And what is my young Irish genius up to now?"

Terry felt himself blush and hoped no one had noticed.

"Still hammering out the pieces," Terry said. "And trying to get the book rolling."

Elaine patted him on the back of his hand.

"Well, if your book is half as good as the piece you did

11

on Thaddeus last year in *Rolling Stone*, it'll be a best seller."

"Hear, hear," said Thaddeus. "Terry will make us all look like pikers."

"Yeah, it'll be great," Joey Gardello said, his dark eyes flashing. "If young Terry ever gets past page thirty-five!"

They all laughed but Terry felt like reaching across the table and strangling Joey. It was just like him to bring up his snail-like pace on the book. Though Terry usually got along with Joey, of late their relationship had soured a little. It was like he was jealous of Thaddeus and Terry being so close. Which was ridiculous. Thaddeus still made time for Joey. It was just that he and Thaddeus were both writers. They had so much in common. Joey was Thaddeus' oldest friend, though. That would never change. Thaddeus and Joey had both grown up in the Bronx. They'd been childhood friends since elementary school. They had even planned on working together someday. Perhaps they'd adapt one of Thaddeus' bestsellers. As kids they used to hang out night and day and talk about how famous they'd become but only one of them had made it. It was tough on Joey. Terry tried to understand that when Joey gave him a hard time.

"Hey, Terry, Terry, you still with us?"

Terry looked across the table and saw Thaddeus laughing at him. Behind him were...Jesus. Behind him were Norman Mailer and Jose Torres on the way out.

"Terry, I want you to meet Norman," Thaddeus said, a devilish grin on his face. He knew exactly how much Terry revered Mailer. The great writer had been his hero since he first read *The Naked* and The Dead when he was a college kid.

"Hey," Terry said, thankful that his voice hadn't

cracked. "It's a pleasure to meet you, Mr. Mailer."

Mailer smiled and shook his hand and introduced him to Jose Torres.

Torres' huge hand enveloped Terry's.

"Thaddeus tells me you're going to be a hell of a novelist," Mailer said.

"That's very generous of him," Terry said. "To tell you the truth you're the reason I wanted to be a writer. I love your work, sir."

"That right?" Mailer said. "I'm the one who got you into this lousy racket? Well, all I can say if that's the truth, then you better be good. 'Cause I don't want to inspire any hacks."

"You've gone and done it now," Mailer said to Thaddeus. "Got yourself famous. Now all you need to do is keep it up for the next forty years or so. It's easy. Like Red Smith said, all it takes to be a writer is sit down and open a vein."

Everyone laughed again, especially Elaine, as Mailer and Torres waved good-bye.

Terry felt electricity sweeping through him. Norman Mailer talking to him, encouraging him. And it was all because he'd profiled Thaddeus, they'd hit it off and Thad had invited him to a dinner party at his girlfriend, the model Shelby Jones', place.

Terry barely had time to revel in meeting Mailer when he felt a tap on his back. When he turned around there were a pair of gorgeous green eyes looking down at him. It was the young actress Valerie Stevenson. Valerie had just been in her first movie, a low budget space opera called *Starcrazy*. The movie was lousy, but she'd gotten good reviews playing a comic and very sexy "creature" from another planet.

"Hi, Terry," she said. "Are you getting hideously drunk?"

"Yeah," Terry said. "I'm competing with Hunter Thompson for the title of most reckless human on the planet. Loved you in the space movie by the way."

"Oh, you saw it?"

"Yeah, Thaddeus and I went to a screening last night. You're my kind of monster."

She laughed and shook her gorgeous hair.

"I'm so glad you liked it. But let's face it, it sucked and I was awful."

"Not at all," Terry said. "That's not true. You can drain all my blood any time."

He reached over, right next to Mick Jagger, and pulled over a chair for her. Mick looked at him and winked. (Oh my God, Mick winked at him! Mick! No, no, he had to be cool about it.)

Valerie set down and looked at him with her adorable green eyes and her perfect lips. Christ, he could feel his heart melting.

"You look great tonight, Terry," Valerie said, folding and unfolding a napkin.

"No, you do, Val," Terry said.

She sighed, reached over, patted him on the cheek and then gave him a tired smile and said, "I'm exhausted. Been on a Vogue shoot in the Bahamas and we worked endless hours. Man, I'm dragging. I have a little blow. You want to sneak back to the men's room with me?"

"Ah, the requisite powder," Terry said. "Well, only a cad would let you sniff all by your lonesome. Let us be gone."

They walked to the other side of the restaurant, the side all the regulars called "Siberia." It was almost as bad to be seated there as it was to only be allowed at the bar. Strictly

B and T Land. The only time anyone from the Star side came into Siberia was to use the bathroom. The clientele was exactly like the people at the bar. Guys in leisure suits and women in bad knockoff dresses stared at them as they walked by.

Terry knew he was supposed to feel superior to them but as he walked down the aisle, he thought how much they looked like the people he'd grown up with in Baltimore. People he had loved all his life. Hard working families who were just here for a little change, a little excitement. The truth was he could probably sit down and chat with any of them and have a perfectly good time. But if he did, he'd be considered a traitor by the celeb class.

And that was the class he aspired to join, wasn't it?

Confused, and turned on by Valerie's legs and amazing ass, he managed to get to the two bathrooms without a further conscience attack. Valerie looked at him and laughed.

"This will blow their minds."

She turned and waved to the diners who looked at them in awe as the two of them went into the men's room together.

Terry opened the slatted door to the toilet, and they crowded in together. Valerie took out her vial of cocaine and shoved a spoon of the white flake under Terry's left nostril. He snorted it in and waited for a second. Then she did the same to his right nostril and by the time he had finished that, he was blasted.

Oh, man, good cocaine. Very good cocaine. Was there anything better? He wondered if Valerie had copped this stuff from Joey. Probably. He felt jacked up, juiced but clearheaded too. He watched as she did the same for herself.

They were both stoned out of their minds and he looked

at her green eyes and her perfect skin and he couldn't help himself. He pulled her to him, and she didn't resist.

They kissed, mashing their bodies against one another. Terry touched her breast, felt pleasantly out of his mind. God, she was so soft, smelled so great. He went lower, rubbing her flat stomach. Lower still. She was moaning, biting his upper lip.

"Hmm, if you tasted any better, you'd be as illegal as the powder," Terry laughed. He tried to kiss her again, but she pushed him back.

"I can't. Terry. Not in here. But I really like you."

Terry kissed her again, but she pushed him away.

"No, I really can't. What if Joey came in?"

"Joey? You dating him?"

"I have been, yes. But he's too crazy. And he's still involved with his ex-wife, Rosalie Torres. He told me they were history but that was bullshit. He can't make a move without consulting her. Just like his great movie career. He had money to make a thriller last year, but he got into a fight with his investors and they pulled out. Really, the only thing cool about him is he's Thaddeus' best friend."

"Yeah, I know," Terry said. "Street bros."

"He can be a violent asshole sometimes. I wouldn't want him to see you with me."

"Hey," Terry said, laughing and making a fist. "I can take care of fucking Joey."

"Really? You don't seem like a tough guy," she said. "You seem like a nice boy with a big talent who is going places."

Terry laughed.

"From your lips to God's ears."

"Another time," Valerie said. They both took another

hit of coke, straightened up in the mirror and headed back out to Siberia. Before they opened the door, Terry kissed her again.

"When can I see you again, Val?"

"I'm doing a modeling gig in the village for the next couple of days. At High Gloss Fashions. It's right across the street from the Lone Star Café, the Tex-Mex place with the giant lizard on the roof. Why don't you drop by?"

"Count me in, kid."

When they went outside, the Fame Hounds watched their every move. Stoned, Terry no longer felt much sympathy for them. Their mouths dropped open, their eyes glossy with longing and jealousy; he wanted to get away from them as soon as possible. He and Valerie slipped back into the other side with the rich, famous and wasted. Where he almost felt at home.

She pressed his hand and whispered in his ear.

"Look, I have to go up front alone, okay? I need to talk to Bruno Veneto."

"The director?"

"Yeah," she said. "He might want me in a movie he's doing soon. But you're irresistible, Terry. See you at the shoot. Or call me. But stay away from Joey. He told me he would kill anyone who got near me."

"Fuck him," Terry said. "You're talking to the Muhammad Ali of ink-stained wretches."

She smiled, touched his cheek and then was gone. Off to see Bruno and further her career.

As he made his way back to Thaddeus' table, he could barely believe any of this had happened. The whole mad scenario which had been so intense just a minute ago now seemed like an illusion. Had he really just done coke and made out with Valerie Stevenson? Did she really like him? Or did he imagine the whole thing? The speed of the transaction and the quality of the coke made it all seem like a fantasy.

He watched as Bruno, the heavy-set director from Rome, kissed her cheek and enveloped her in his big arms. From feeling incredibly lucky Terry now felt a kind of emptiness in the pit of his stomach. Only minutes ago, he was ready to fall in love.

Who was she? What game were they playing? Who the fuck could tell?

Valerie was nodding seriously to everything Bruno was saying. But Terry tried not to get resentful or weird about it. That was the square, old fashioned way of seeing things, his old self reacting to life in New York in the fast lane like some hick from the Finger Lakes.

He sat down next to Elaine, stoned, wired, but underneath, suddenly exhausted.

Where the fuck was he? Who the fuck was he?

He didn't know anymore...

Joey Gardello smiled at him in his reptilian manner.

"Where have you been, professor?" he said.

"Took a little trip to Siberia."

"With Valerie?"

Should he admit it to Joey? Yeah, why not? Fuck Joey.

"Yeah, what of it?"

"Leave her alone," Joey said. "She's spoken for."

"Funny, she doesn't seem to think so."

Joey looked at him like he wanted to rip Terry's head off.

"Watch your step, Terry," he said. "You're strictly a lightweight."

"Really? Remind me. What's the name of your new

movie?"

Joey threw back his chair and came around the table.

"Listen to me, Terry. I'm going to marry that girl. As soon as my deal comes through."

"You'd need more than a deal to get Valerie, Joe," Terry said. "You'd need a whole new personality."

"Fuck you, you low life journalist. You stay the fuck away from her, you hear me!"

He moved toward Terry in a menacing way, but Thaddeus quickly interrupted.

"Boys, boys. This is just the coke and booze talking."

Joey bit his lip and sat down.

"We aren't done yet, Brennan."

"Anytime, Joe."

He sat down and took a hit of whiskey to take the edge off the coke. Then in his ear he heard: "I'm beginning to think Joey Gardello is becoming a bullying wannabe mobster."

Terry turned and saw horn-rimmed, brown-haired Gina Wade, Thaddeus's assistant and chief researcher. Gina lived in the East Village, Tomkins Square Park, wrote book reviews for *The New York Review* and brilliant left-wing think pieces for the *Voice*. She even did some reviews for the *New York Times*. Though she was shy and withdrawn most of the time, she perked right up whenever Thaddeus was around.

She sat down next to Terry, smiled and kissed him on the cheek.

"You're looking incredibly stoned," she said.

"I am incredibly stoned," Terry said. "Too stoned to be hip."

Across the table Joey got up in a dramatic way, swirling

his coat around like a nineteenth century cavalry officer, before putting it on. He glowered again at Terry.

"Remember what I said, professor," he said. "Valerie is with me."

Then he turned and made his way through the crowd.

"He's being particularly irritating tonight," Gina said. "Did you step on his fantasy?"

"Yeah, I think so," Terry said, laughing. "Though I'm not sure which one."

She smiled and took out a novel from her purse. It was her favorite trick. Reading a novel while all around her the celebs cavorted.

"What is the genius reading now?" Terry said, kissing her back on the cheek. In her own academic, nerdy way, she was adorable.

"Firbank again," she said. She showed Terry an ancient copy of *The Flower Beneath the Foot.*

"Better you than me," Terry said. "I tried Firbank in my early aesthete years, but I couldn't understand that level of campiness."

Gina smiled and punched Terry playfully on the arm.

"Liar," she said.

Terry laughed and shook his head.

"How's kicks?"

But she wasn't talking to him anymore. Instead she was looking at Thaddeus, who was nuzzling up to Shelby Jones, who had just made an appearance. Shelby of the raven hair, awesome cheekbones, and dark, gorgeous eyes. She was dressed in a flowing silver Halston gown and looked every inch the equal of the movie stars in the room. Gina's eyes flickered with pain.

Everyone knew that the true love of Gina's life was

Thaddeus Bryant. A love, Terry thought, that was doomed. Not that it was Thaddeus' fault. He was charming with her, of course, but that was his nature. He charmed everyone, male and female. For the first time Terry thought of how much Gina was like Joey. They were both smitten attendants to King Thad. Though she wasn't bitter and vicious about it. Instead, she just stiffened as Thaddeus put his arms around the gorgeous Shelby and kissed her on her perfect little ear.

"The place is really hopping tonight," Gina said. "Just think if a bomb went off in here. The loss to American society would be negligible. In the end what you would have is a lot of expensive coffins and the world would mourn for all of ten minutes."

"Oh, I think longer than that, Gina," Terry said. "I'd say up to but not beyond one day."

Thaddeus broke away from Shelby and came over to Gina. He reached down and picked her up in both arms and twirled her around like a large doll.

"My heart, my soul," he said. "How are you, dear?"

"Better now," she said. She was smiling so widely that it looked as though a switch had flicked on inside of her.

"I have all the research you need," she said.

"Wonderful. We'll work on it tomorrow afternoon."

He ordered Gina a drink, then turned to Terry.

"Want to go out for some air?" Thaddeus said, smiling at him kindly.

"Lead the way," Terry said.

"Don't run away or I'll have to spank you," Gina said.

"Hmmm," Thaddeus said, and kissed her cheek. Gina sat down and picked up her Firbank. She looked happy now, like an A student reading in the stacks.

21

* * *

Terry managed to climb from his chair to follow Thaddeus outside, but he was interrupted by Howard Freeman, a fellow journalist. Howard was a scholarly type who wrote pieces on mysticism and other fading countercultural pastimes. He lived in a constant state of panic about his failing career. More than once Terry had taken calls from him saying he was going to throw himself on the subway tracks. In fact, only two weeks ago he had talked Howard down from jumping off of his apartment roof in Chelsea. Howard was a pain in the ass but a good friend too, the kind of guy who had rock solid values. So what if he was an old hippie, Terry thought. So was he. At least in the 1960s people stood up for one another. Now Howard looked bombed out of his mind. His prematurely white hair was uncombed and stood up in tufts all over his head. He reminded Terry of Gyro Gearloose, the mad professor in Donald Duck comics. Howard threw an arm around Terry.

"My buddy," he said. "There aren't many of us left now, Ter."

"That's right," Terry said, instantly uncomfortable. "We are the last of the breed."

Ugh. Suddenly, he wished Howard would disappear in a puff of smoke. It was one thing to be an old hippie but when you started talking about it, it sounded false, in a self-congratulatory kind of way.

"Tell you, Ter, I wouldn't be where I am today without your help. Thanks so much for introducing me to Jimmy Walker at *Rolling Stone*. He's a good guy, interested in me writing for them. Woulda' never met him without you, Ter."

He hugged Terry and Terry could smell his bad breath and his sweaty fear.

"That's okay, Howard. He's the lucky one."

"Anytime I can help you, Terry. Anything I can do."

Howard stopped and got a serious look on his face.

"What is it, Howie?"

"Tell you the truth, I was a little angry at you, Ter. But you know me. I can't stay mad."

"What? What did I do?"

"You forgot my birthday party the other night. We held it here. It was great. I just missed you, man."

"Shit, Howie. I am sorry," Terry said. He remembered now. He and Thaddeus had been out late at this big publishing party and then went downtown to the Odeon. He had never given a thought to Howard.

"It's fine. I know you have bigger things to do these days."

"No, man. I was just confused. I've already bought you an amazing present. I'll give it to you this weekend."

Howard brightened up and hugged Terry again.

"That's great, Ter. Thanks. You're the best."

"You too, Howard."

"Can you give me a hint what it is?"

"No hints, Howard." Especially when he had no idea what the hell it was. He'd have to buy something tomorrow.

"Listen, Terry, I wanted to tell you something."

"So tell away."

"That girl, Valerie. She's great looking but be careful. I hear she's a real player."

Terry felt a bolt of anger. He didn't want fucking Howard's lame advice. What the fuck did Howard know about her? Nothing at all. He had to stop himself from lashing out at his old buddy.

"Thanks, bud," Terry said. "I'll keep that in mind."

"We just have to watch out for one another, you know?"

"Right. We do."

Howard gave Terry an awkward hug then then slipped away, heading for Carly Simon, who had just strolled in the door. Good, let Carly deal with his endless celeb worship.

Terry watched Howard throw his arms around her and smother her face with alcoholic kisses. As he saw Carly sweetly push Howard away, Terry remembered another Howard, a committed revolutionary who had for a time seriously thought of joining the Weathermen. A guy who had sworn he would spend his life living in the East Village in poverty rather than chase the bitch goddess of success.

Where had that guy gone?

As Terry headed toward the front door, past the Bridge and Tunnel Crowd at the bar, all the heads turned toward him, and he heard the fat guy say: "That guy is somebody. Think he's an actor. Or something." Terry turned and looked at Big Clarence, who stared back at him with worshipful eyes. Terry felt a small shock inside and then anger. Whether it was superficial or not, he had to admit he really wanted the bar crowd to know his name and what he had written. It mattered to him...more and more every day. Was that good or bad? He wasn't sure. Only that it was true. Suddenly, as he followed Thaddeus outside, he recalled a novel he had once wanted to write about steelworkers he knew back in Baltimore. He had shown the beginning to Howard, who had really supported him and thought the book was wonderful. But he had also shown it to a couple of editors who said it was old-fashioned, 1930s proletariat fiction. They could never sell it to their houses' editorial boards. So he'd put it aside. That was two years ago. He'd told himself that he'd get back to it, but the truth was he would probably never look at it again.

Cabs and limousines waited outside Elaine's as a light fall rain came down. Thaddeus took out his pack of Lucky Strikes and lit one up. He offered one to Terry who shook his head.

"Fucking Joey," Thaddeus said. "I heard him hassling you. He's having a tough time right now. The truth is he's kind of mad at me, but he can't say that, so he picks on you."

"Why's he pissed at you?"

"It's too boring to talk about. His career is stalled and he's jealous of my success. Says I'm not there for him. In some ways he's right. I've been busy as hell. I haven't had time to deal with him."

"And let me guess, he thinks you should be spending all your free time with him. The two of you should be up in the Bronx terrorizing the Fordham Road."

"Something like that. Look, I've known him all my life, and he's a good guy. Very talented but he lets the small stuff get in his way. He's got a terrible temper and after a certain age people don't forgive you for that kind of shit anymore."

Terry nodded.

"You want my opinion, I think it's amazing that you're still loyal to him at all."

"I tell myself I'm helping him, but I'm not sure I am."

"Maybe you should try some of the old 'benign neglect' of J. Patrick Moynihan."

Thaddeus smiled.

"Maybe I should. We have a long and tortured history. But your boyhood pals are still your boyhood pals. Know what I mean?"

"Not exactly."

Thaddeus bit his lower lip and got a strange, unreadable look on his face.

"He had my back when we were kids. Joey was a tough guy, watched out for me."

Terry shook his head. Then the rain came down and made him feel like he was in a film noir.

"But that's neither here nor there. I just want you to know you're a hell of a writer," Thaddeus said. "And I know you can make it. You just need to work hard and believe in yourself."

"Thanks, T," Terry said. "That means a lot to me. Though this isn't the right time, I wanted to ask you if... ah...you've had time to look at the pages I gave you from *Bad Boy*?"

"I have," Thaddeus said. "But do we really want to stand out here in the rain discussing them?"

"No, I guess not but...well, could you tell me what you think in a general way? It's driving me crazy."

Thaddeus laughed and affectionately patted Terry on the shoulder.

"All right. In two seconds, I have this to say. The writing is brilliant, but a little too sarcastic. You need to have compassion for your characters. Even the nastiest ones. If you have that, people will follow you anywhere. I can be more specific when we go over it. Out of the rain, you fanatic!"

Terry tried to laugh but felt a sinking feeling. He had already suspected that this would be Thaddeus' attitude. In his own work Thaddeus could describe the biggest jerk in the world but with a compassion that made you understand, if not love, him.

"Your pieces are usually snappy and tough minded, which is fine," Thaddeus said. "But in a novel people expect more."

Terry nodded, and suddenly the rain felt colder, wetter.

"But this is nothing you can't fix Terry," Thaddeus said. "You've got the chops; now just work on heightening the emotions in your story. Remember, even villains feel they're right."

Terry sighed deeply.

"You're right, of course. How's the movie coming?"

"They wrapped three days ago, and I hear the editing is going well. Hoffman is supposed to be great in it."

"Wow," Terry said. "That's fantastic."

"Yeah, but don't count on it until the line forms at the box office. That's where it counts. Hey, I'm glad Valerie Stevenson seems to dig you, Ter."

"Oh, come on," Terry said. "She's just playing with me. Sort of like a cat plays with a mouse before he claws it to death."

"That's where you're wrong. Girls in her class don't waste time playing."

"Now that you mention it, class is the problem. She's like about four classes above me. Where am I going to take her for a dinner? Spark Steak House? The Lion's Head?"

"Why not? She'd probably dig hanging out with the scribes down in the Village. Speaking of which, you still sweet on that barmaid in there, what's her name?"

"Kathy," Terry said. "Kathy Anderson."

"And you prefer Kathy to Valerie?"

"Valerie? Come on. I'm a diversion for her. She's on her way to live with some billionaire on a yacht. Maybe she'll hire me as their deckhand."

Even as he said it, Terry hoped it wasn't true.

Then he thought of Kathy. Her smile. Her easy way with him.

"Let me ask you a question?" Thaddeus said. As he spoke, he pulled out the switchblade knife he always carried with him. He revealed it to very few people. Terry had asked him about it when he'd done his piece for *Rolling Stone*, and Thaddeus had said that he started carrying it when he was robbed by gang members in the Bronx. The Fordham Baldies.

"I've never used it," he'd said. "Then, or, obviously, now. But just having it makes me feel safe. And I know how to use it. Trust me."

Now Terry watched as he flicked it open and shut.

"Why did you give up your nice little life in cozy Geneva, New York, and come to live in big, bad New York City?"

Terry rubbed his jaw and felt breathless. God, he hated to be interrogated by Thaddeus. Even if it was for his own good.

"To have adventure, find fame, fortune. Romance."

"Exactly. So why would you tie yourself down to some little barmaid who has the exact same values you left behind?"

"No, she doesn't. She's only working as a barmaid for the time being. She's an actress and a good one. I saw her in an Off-Broadway version of *Mother Courage* and she was..."

Thaddeus laughed, put away his knife into his inner jacket pocket, and put his arm around Terry's neck.

"I met her...Remember? You and I went to the Head and we traded quips with Kathy for two hours. She's very cute, she's very sweet. She's going to make some guy in New Jersey a very nice wife and mother. 'Cause after she gives up acting, in about a year, she'll move back there, meet some local bar band rocker, and soon they'll have two or three kids. That will be it for his fantasy, too, and after he quits pretending, he's Bruce Springsteen he'll get a job managing an Arby's. Then comes the nifty little white clapboard bungalow with a swing set in the back yard. And every once in a while, they'll think back to when she wasn't forty pounds overweight and he wasn't a suburban alcoholic."

Terry felt like Thaddeus had stabbed him in the chest.

And this after just telling him he needed more compassion for his characters.

"Man, you are so cynical sometimes, Thad. You don't know any of this. She could get a break. Become a star."

"No, she can't and she won't. Look at her. Does she have Valerie's bone structure, does she walk like a star, does she have the right voice? The best she could be is, ah...this generation's Joan Blondell, and this generation doesn't have a fucking Joan Blondell. Get it?"

Terry wanted to be pissed off at Thaddeus, but the Joan Blondell line was so funny he had to laugh.

"So, I'm a hopeless plebian," he said.

"No, you just want to be with someone you can feel superior to. But you're at the turning point now, my boy. You need to resist the urge to fall in love with someone who reminds you of your childhood home in good old row house Baltimore and take on more challenging women. The greater the risk, the bigger the reward."

"You make it sound like I should treat life like I'm some kind of pirate."

"Actually, that's an excellent way of looking at it. Moving up in the world requires the skills of an artist in your writing but also the stealth and courage of a pirate in your life. Yo ho ho and over the side with our scabbards, boys!"

Thaddeus assumed an Errol Flynn pose and pretended to run Terry through with his knife.

Terry dodged out of his way and practically fell into the street.

They both ended up laughing and holding one another up.

"Shall we go back inside for some more cheap thrills?" Thaddeus said.

"Nah," Terry said, suddenly feeling exhausted. "Gotta go pitch a new piece at *Stone* tomorrow. Might be good if I was awake."

"I hear you, kid, "Thaddeus said. "Here, take that limo instead of a cab. I'm in a rare unselfish mood and I'll grab the tab."

Terry smiled, shook his head.

"No way. I'll take a cab."

"Nonsense," Thaddeus said. "Travel first class. It's the only way to go."

He practically shoved Terry into an empty limo, then leaned in and spoke to the driver.

"Take this scabby scribe down to the West Village and see that he doesn't stop in at the Lion's Head either. There awaits his doom!"

He threw a hundred bucks at the driver, tapped Terry

on the head and shut the door behind him.

Terry fell back into the luxurious leather seat and immediately felt his body relax.

It was so comfortable, and he had just hung out with some of the coolest people in the world, people most of the rest of the world could only see in the movies or concerts. He knew he should appreciate it, dig it. He had come to New York for adventures and success and he was having his share of both of them. So why worry?

Before he shut his eyes, he took one last look at Elaine's. The crowd headed in, filled with celebrities. Was that Jackie Bisset? Maybe she and Julie Christie could have a beauty contest.

And then, suddenly, at the window was the big man from the bar. Clarence himself, watching Terry's every move.

Yeah, it was the fat guy who was out of the loop. The fat guy who would do anything to be able to sit with the stars. Terry suddenly felt sorry for him. The poor guy, living out a fantasy life, like so many other saps in the world.

He was lucky. He really was.

And yet, for some reason he couldn't quite understand, he was going home early to crawl into bed.

CHAPTER THREE

1976-Two Years Earlier

Terry loved Thaddeus Bryant's book *The Debt*. A book about four friends who had taken different paths in the 1960s. One of them, Max, became a soldier, a Green Beret, and lost his right arm. His best friend Mike became a rocker but succumbed to heroin. James' girlfriend, Lake, had gone to Marin and lived in a commune, a dream that sustained her for a while but in the end had fallen apart. The fourth member of their group was their college professor at Yale, Professor Walter Hicks, and it was he who had sent them all on their way. Professor Hicks with his leftist dreams of utopia. All of them owed him a debt of some kind, but each of them interpreted this debt in a different way.

After the war they had gotten back together in New York for a summer of fun and relaxation in the Hamptons and it was there that their real relationships revealed themselves. The novel was both comic and tragic and all of it realized with a sensitivity and intelligence that startled both critics and readers.

Frankly, Terry couldn't believe that Thaddeus had pulled it off. The book everyone wanted to write. A freaking classic.

He was surprised when Jim Walker had agreed to let him interview Thaddeus for *Rolling Stone*. *Stone* seldom profiled authors. But Walker, who hung out at Elaine's, knew and admired Thaddeus Bryant and had thought personable and idealistic Terry and the brilliant, bestselling Thaddeus Bryant would be a perfect match.

Terry had done many celebrity interviews over the past year and a half, but this one really made him nervous. He realized, as he planned what he would ask, that he not only wanted to do a good job on the story but somehow hoped that he and Thaddeus Bryant would become friends.

On the first day of their interview they met at the Museum of Modern Art. Thaddeus wore a brown leather jacket, a grey-blue cotton shirt, dark wool pants and expensive Gucci loafers. With his thick brown Kennedyesque hair, classic WASP features and twice broken nose, Thaddeus looked as handsome as a film star but as rugged as the Marlboro man. Terry reminded himself to get the label of Thaddeus' jacket, since he knew nothing about fashion. Of course, he couldn't actually afford one, but maybe he could one day, when he finished his novel and some young journalist was writing pieces about him. Now he had to content himself with the Official New York Freelance Writer Uniform. He wore a black T-shirt, black Levi's, black socks, a beat-up black leather jacket, and Jack Purcell's. He looked like one of the Ramones, but truth be told, he felt a felt little shoddy as he stood there in front of Jackson Pollack's *Full Fathom Five*. Like a lost teenager standing with a full-fledged adult.

"You see, he has crushed cigarettes glued on here,"

Thaddeus said, pointing at the painting.

Terry had seen nothing but squiggly lines and drips. He looked closer and found something himself.

"Look here, thumbtacks glued on and what's this? A key."

"I love it," Thaddeus said. "And people said he couldn't paint."

"Yeah, it's pretty amazing," Terry agreed. Usually he didn't know what to think about any of the Abstract Expressionists. Sometimes he felt like he did today, that they were geniuses. Other days he felt they were gigantic frauds. On those days he longed to look at Edward Hopper, or, God help him, Norman Rockwell. His tastes (if they could even be called "tastes") were ill-formed. He had never studied art in school and wasn't sure what to think about any of it. He hid his massive ignorance of the art world behind a scrim of quick humor. It usually got him through.

Thaddeus smiled at him now, as if he were reading Terry's confused mind.

"Be honest," he said. "You don't really think sticking a cigarette butt on a bunch of blotches is great art, do you?"

"I don't know," Terry said. He was mortified that Thaddeus had called his bluff and hoped he wasn't blushing.

But Thaddeus' smile changed from challenging to compassionate.

"Hell, I don't know either. I'm not sure anyone does. But on my good days, when I feel like being understanding to old Jackson, I'd say that you have to see his work as sort of Mind Explosions, pictures of violent emotions, or mood swings. Some are calming, some crazy, maybe even suicidal or murderous."

Terry had never thought of the paintings that way before.

"States of consciousness," he said. "That's interesting."

"Thanks," Thaddeus said. "Of course, it might just all be bullshit. But maybe that's what all art is, part angelic, part hustle."

They both laughed and Terry felt a rush of warmth for him. He wasn't pretentious at all. It occurred to him that Thaddeus had as many doubts about "Great Art" as he did, but, unlike himself, Thaddeus felt perfectly confident in displaying his ambivalence.

"I do know one thing, though, for sure," Thaddeus said. "There's something sexy about Pollack's paintings. They give off a great amount of emotion, like Kerouac's writing, you know? Seeing this great ejaculation makes me want to pick up a woman and have my way with her."

He nodded toward a red-haired woman in tight jeans and an even tighter midnight blue blouse standing across the room. She was staring at a great red Rothko.

Terry wrote Thaddeus' reaction down on his pad of paper. A perfect moment for his piece.

"You think she wants to have sex with you?" he said.

"Absolutely," Thaddeus said. Normally Terry would have found this attitude unbearably arrogant, like something from the mouth of the actor he least liked, Warren Beatty, but Thaddeus didn't sound arrogant at all. His voice was amused and seemed to include his journalist friend in his little game.

"Look at her," Thaddeus said. "Don't you see what I mean?"

Terry dared to look at her straight on and saw that her eyes were wide open and her red lips seemed to quiver in sexual excitement.

Or was he only imagining that?

In any case, he felt excited himself. There was no denying the electricity in the room.

"I could have her right now," Thaddeus said. His lips were thick, like Jagger's, and now there was a savage lust in his eyes.

Terry laughed.

"Just because she's flirting with you doesn't mean she'd actually make love to you," he said.

"True," Thaddeus smiled. "So let's find out."

With that he started to walk across the room. Terry trailed just behind him, wondering what Thaddeus' opening gambit would be.

But he never found out for as they got closer the red-haired woman with the porcelain skin and red lips smiled and said: "Aren't you Thaddeus Bryant, the author of *The Debt*?"

"Why yes," Thaddeus said, giving her his warmest smile.

"I'm Ellen James. I work right around the corner at Tweed."

"Ah, a terrific shop. I know several women who shop there."

"I'm sure you do," she said.

"This is my friend, Terry Brennan, from *Rolling Stone*," Thaddeus said.

She smiled politely at Terry, but her eyes went back to Thaddeus in a flash. Now Terry could see that he'd been right. Her bottom lip was quivering, and she looked as though she were about to go down on her knees.

"Do you come here often, Ellen?" Thaddeus asked.

"A couple days a week," she said. "But not lately. Lately I've been spending my lunch hour reading your novel."

"That is so kind of you to say," Thaddeus said.

"I love it," she said. She sounded awestruck.

"Ellen," Thaddeus said. "Perhaps we could meet and have a drink one day later this week?"

"Yes, that would be nice," she said. The words were cool, but it was obvious she was thrilled. She almost dropped her fashionable little handbag as she fished for her business card.

"My home number is on here too," she said.

"Great," Thaddeus said. "We have to go now. But it's been a pleasure."

Thaddeus took her by her shoulders and kissed her on the cheek. Terry could hear a sigh of longing that almost made him laugh out loud.

Outside of the museum Thaddeus spoke in a mock professorial manner: "Well, now, students, I think we have learned something very valuable today."

"And what is that, sir?" Terry said, playing along.

"We have learned what abstract expressionism is really about," he said. "We have learned that this great and confusing artistic movement gets you laid. And what higher goal can any art achieve?"

"Let me get that down for the final exam," Terry said, pretending to scribble in his notebook.

As they both cracked up and walked down Fifth Avenue, Terry listened to Thaddeus's witty comments on the fashionable denizens of the street. Though he was usually cool toward the people he wrote about, he felt something much deeper about Thaddeus. They were, after all, close in age, Thaddeus thirty-two and himself thirty, and they seemed to have similar sensibilities, though Thaddeus's was much more advanced. Still, just being with him gave Terry the feeling that they were brothers in arms. Thaddeus had published exactly one short story, the germ of the idea for *The Debt* and then, two years later, had stunned the world with his brilliance and passion. The novel had the immediacy of Kerouac's prose, but also something else that Kerouac could have never done. That is, it had a wonderful plot with reversals and reveals that reminded the reader of Dickens.

Just the kind of book Terry wanted to write.

And now, inspired by Thaddeus, maybe he would be able to actually carry on and finish it.

Far from merely being a subject he wrote about for *Rolling Stone*, Terry felt that Thaddeus and he were guerilla fighters in a life and death battle against fakery, boredom and the disco dullness of their time. Of course, he realized he was jumping the gun on all this. There was still the possibility that Thaddeus was just being a good subject for the piece. But it didn't feel that way. Not at all. And as they walked on, into Central Park, he hoped that they were headed toward a deep and lasting artistic friendship.

CHAPTER FOUR

1978

Rosalie Torres had never been in a morgue before, though she had seen a thousand of them on the cop shows that Joey liked to watch on TV. Now, standing here, waiting for the coroner to open the door where the bodies were laid out on steel tables, she felt a weird déjà vu, like she'd seen Joey's dead body before and this was just an instant replay. That was so wrong, she thought. When your lover dies you should feel something unique, something deep and real inside, not like you're a character in a cheap TV movie. On the other hand, isn't that what she felt now about everything? Her entire life felt like a replay from a bad movie. It hadn't always been that way. She didn't even like movies when she first met Joey. She found them dull, obvious, and dumb. She didn't like the stars or the stories they told. Especially the crime stories. The guys who wrote them, mostly kids from some Ivy League school, obviously knew nothing about crime at all.

What they knew they learned on television. Maybe Joey wasn't the genius he claimed to be, but at least he was from the Bronx and knew something about the real mean streets.

That was his strength: he knew what the hell he was writing about. But his weaknesses, well, he had so many. The main one being his arrogance and tough guy attitude. Rosalie knew that it was only a cover for his fear, his lack of education. Most of the kids he was up against in the film biz were from wealthy homes, had every advantage. All Joey had was his talent and attitude. It took him pretty far. He had some fans among the money men in the biz. But, in the end, they were afraid to back him. Nobody really trusted a crazy kid like Joey to direct a big expensive movie. They loved getting high with him at Elaine's. But finally, they felt he was too street, too crazy, too impulsive.

Sadly, Rosalie thought, as Joey became more desperate, instead of toning down his act, he brought it up a few notches. He called people assholes, laughed at their bourgeois pretensions. He had started to believe he was some kind of Mafia goon. He bought his own bullshit and now he was gone for good.

And so was his brother Ray. Jesus, Ray, who worked odd jobs, his last one being a pizza chef at Angelo's Pizza on Fordham Road.

What was he doing with Joey in the park at that hour?

She didn't have to wonder what Joey was doing. He was dealing drugs like he usually did three days a week. But Ray...that didn't make sense. Unless Joey somehow talked Ray into some scam. Something which got them both killed.

"Miss," a voice said.

She looked up and saw two New York detectives and a doctor in a white lab coat staring down at her.

"Yes?"

"You here to identify Joseph Gardello?" the doctor said.

"Yes," she said, hearing her own hollow voice.

"I'm Detective Green," the black one said, "and this is Detective Lazenby." He pointed to his thin white partner, with a crew cut and white hair. They both showed her their ID's. "This is the medical examiner, Doctor Weaver."

"Rosalie Torres," she said. And then wondered how they had known who she was here to see.

Weaver was an older man with skin the color of grey crepe soles nodded his skinny, bald head. She got up and walked between the two cops.

Both of the cops held her up in a gentle way, and she felt an outsized gratitude to them. What wonderful men, what a kind and gentle place is the morgue.

She barely heard the Medical Examiner's technical description of the wounds. Anyway, they were all too obvious. Two bullets in the chest, two bullets which pierced his aorta and killed him within ten seconds. What really tortured her was Joey's face. He looked basically just like himself, only kind of whitish blue. That was the weird thing. Like he'd put on some powder to maybe play a small Hitchcockian role in one of his own unmade movies.

"Is that Joseph Gardello?"

"Yeah. That's him." Her voice sounded like a monotone from a movie. She hated it.

They moved to the next body and the doc took off the sheet. Ray didn't look as good as Joey. His head had basically exploded like an old pomegranate she'd seen dropped from a second story window in junior high school.

"That Ray Gardello?"

"Yes."

The doctor made a scribble on a form.

"Thank you," he said. "That's all. If you can just sign this."

* * *

Later, outside, the two cops talked to her. They were friendly in a cop kind of way. Green smiled at her and said he was sorry for her loss. Rosalie heard herself say "Thank you."

"A few things we need to know."

"Such as?"

"Such as do you have any idea what Joey Gardello and his older brother, Ray, were doing in the park at two a.m.?"

"No. I guess he couldn't sleep. So maybe he was taking a walk. He did that sometimes. Up and down Broadway. Then he'd dodge into the park."

Now Lazenby stepped up. He had serious garlic breath. Probably had just eaten a slice.

"Taking a walk, huh? Did he always take walks in the freaking park at two a.m.?"

Rosalie looked at him. A scenario came into her head. One she didn't want in there because if you thought about something maybe you had to do something about it. And she didn't want to be involved in solving Joey's murder. She didn't want to do anything at all. Christ, she didn't even want to be here.

"He liked to walk in the park late at night. He could take care of himself."

"Really?" Lazenby said. "You think so?"

"He usually carry a lot of money on him?" Green said.

"No, just twenty bucks," Rosalie said.

"How come just twenty?"

"'Cause he grew up inna Bronx," Rosalie said, using her street dialect to sound like she believed what she was saying. "You carry twenty bucks with you in case the guys wanna roll you. Then you can offer to split it with 'em. Ten for each of you. Sometimes, since you're a good guy, they go for it, leave you ten and don't fuck you up."

"I highly doubt that," Lazenby said.

"Why?" Rosalie said.

"Because what would he do with the other money?" Lazenby asked.

"What *other* money?" she said.

"All the money he made from drug dealing," Green said. "We know your ex-husband was a drug dealer, Rosalie. So you might as well tell us who his supplier was and who he was dealing to, 'cause one of them is probably who shot him."

"Bullshit," Rosalie said.

"We work the park," Lazenby said. "You think this is the first time we seen Joe out there at night?"

"Yeah, well why didn't you bust him, then?" she said.

"That's our business," Green said. "But we know who he deals with, too."

"Is that right?" Rosalie said. "You guys seem to know everything."

"We know he deals with Nicky Baines," Green said.

"Yeah, we figure he might have gotten his big, strong-armed brother to help him steal some dope from one of Nicky's trucks. But they weren't smart enough to pull it off and Nicky whacked 'em both. How's that sound?"

"Sounds like a good story for TV Maybe you guys could send it in to Aaron Spelling?"

The two cops smiled at one another.

"He ever tell you anything about his plans?"

"Yeah, he planned to go see the Giants play in a couple of weeks."

"Cute. But we were referring to stealing dope."

"Or maybe he already stole it and brought it home?"

"I'm separated from him, remember?" Rosalie said. "He doesn't call me up and tell me shit."

"Yeah, but we seen you two together sometimes around the West Side. Maybe you were getting back together. Maybe he was going to use the money he stole to start a new life in paradise with you."

"Yeah, we were moving to Enchanted Island," she said.

Green and Lazenby nodded.

"She's very amusing, isn't she?" Lazenby said.

"Yeah, I have seldom heard a more biting wit," Green said.

"He and his bro got whacked, execution style, Rosalie. Nicky doesn't waste time doing shit like that unless there's a good reason," Lazenby said.

"Yeah," Green said. "He's a gentle soul really who only kills people if he feels personally anguished by their poor behavior."

"Isn't that interesting," Rosalie said.

"We think so," Lazenby said.

"Yeah, we do, "Green said. "You ever meet any of these individuals?"

"What?"

"I got a list of certain types Joseph hung with," Lazenby said. "One is a black man named Willie Hudson. You know him?"

"I met him a few times. He's a bouncer at Studio 54."

"That's right. You think he might be involved in borrowing Nicky's coke?"

"No, I don't."

"When was the last time you seen him?" Lazenby said.

"He and Joey studied acting and directing together at the Strasburg Institute. They got together once in a while and talked about that. Willie is also a movie maker wannabe. He isn't interested in drugs."

"Really?" Green said. "We've heard of individuals who steal drugs and sell them to finance their movies."

"Really?" Rosalie said. "Well, they must be really morons. Joey was no angel, but he was a lot smarter than that."

"Everyone is smart until they get a bad idea," Green said.

"Yeah," Lazenby said. "Ideas are like organic, living things which take on their own lives and certain individuals become mesmerized by them. Even smart individuals, sometimes."

"Well, I wouldn't know about that," said Rosalie. "I'm just a poor Puerto Rican girl who works as a waitress at Florio's restaurant."

"How about this individual?" Lazenby said. "You ever see Joey hanging with him?"

They showed her a picture which made her take an involuntary gulp of breath.

"That's the journalist, Terry Brennan," she said. "He's a friend of Joey's but he's not into drugs or anything else."

"You sound like you know that for sure," Green said.

"You tight with this guy?" Lazenby said.

"No. But he's a guy who is, like, somebody Joey knows from hanging out at Elaine's. You know Elaine's?"

"We've heard of it, but do not traffic with those scum. *Rolling Stone* reporter, right?"

"I guess."

"Like that Hunter Thompson. Always bragging how

they flaunt the law, take drugs."

"Triple hipsters," Green said. "Sort of like Joey, right?"

"Maybe he wanted to write a movie. Maybe they all got involved in ripping off Nicky Baines."

Rosalie laughed.

"You guys really *should* go see Aaron Spelling."

Lazenby gave her his card.

"Thank you, Rosalie. And if you happen to think of anything which could be helpful, please don't hesitate to call."

"Okay," said Rosalie. "Can I go now?"

"Sure. Just be careful. We might not be the only personages looking for the stolen dope."

"This is true," Green said. "And the other people might not be so amusing and polite as we are."

Rosalie felt an electric current of fear pass through her.

Jesus Christ, she thought as she hurried down the cold hallway. "You fuck, Joey. You get killed but that isn't enough. You gotta get me involved in this thing too."

The thought of Nicky Baines' boys showing up at her door made her shudder. She knew that tonight she'd sleep with her .38 next to the bed.

CHAPTER FIVE

Though he had gone home early, Terry still had a serious hangover. His head felt lopsided, like someone had kicked him in the right temple and the whole mass had shifted to the left. His editor at *Rolling Stone*, Jim Walker, sat behind a new steel desk, his legs crossed and his cold blue eyes staring at him through his rimless glasses.

"So," Walker said. "Another evening of wasted potential?"

Terry tried to laugh but any movement of his jaw muscles made him want to cry.

He sat down gingerly on the couch across from the tall, good looking editor.

"Still snorting the old powder?"

"Nah, stuff makes me nutso," Terry lied.

"More nutso," Walker said.

Terry laughed. This was the M.O. at *Stone*. Everyone pretended to be wilder than they really were. Living in the fast lane, teetering on the edge of madness. Barely able to write their dangerous record reviews of criminal outlaw rockers! Oh the terrifying ecstatic madness of it all! But as they moved into their late thirties most of the wild rebel journalists were starting to have some medical problems, or they had ended up in expensive rehab once or twice too often. Yeah, some of them might still live in fleabag apartments in Alphabet City, but by forty Terry was pretty sure they would end up with three kids in the suburbs just like the elder generation they so easily mocked. The unhip generation that had wasted their youth saving the world.

Terry took a breath and readied himself for his "pitch session" with Walker. But Walker seemed distracted, nervously tapping his pencil on his desk and looking out the window.

"You want to hear this now, Jim?"

Walker snapped back to attention in a nervous way, running his right hand through his hair.

"Yeah, sure. What do you have?"

His tone was short, jumpy. Not like the smooth Jim Walker Terry had known for the last two years. Something was definitely bugging him, but whatever it was he wasn't going to share it with Terry.

"Okay," Terry said, moving into his pitch. "I have a couple good things for you."

"Really?" said Walker. "Tell me. I sit here waiting to be stunned."

Terry was again taken aback. Was there a slightly hostile edge to Walker's voice?

Terry was about to talk about a piece he had already set up out West, a visit with Tom McGuane, Warren Oates, and Sam Peckinpah, all of whom were meeting at McGuane's ranch in Livingstone, Montana.

But suddenly he remembered something he actually wanted to do more. Something personal.

"Remember a while back," he said. "When we were drinking down at the Head? We had this great discussion of Haight-Ashbury, the old hippie dream of Utopia and how it related to rock music. I'd like to do a piece, a think piece but with interviews from musicians, of course, about how far rock has strayed from that initial dream, you know? You remember the old days, when *Stone* was still in San Francisco. We all had this idea of a better world. It was what made the music so powerful. Now it seems to have almost disappeared. The piece could be a reminder to our generation what's really important. And maybe it could wake a few of the younger readers up too."

Terry hadn't expected to say that. Nothing of that nature had even been in his mind on the way up to the *Stone* offices. It was as though the whole thing had sprung from his deeper soul, some place he tried to hide from other people for fear they would find him corny or ridiculous.

Walker drank some of his coffee and sighed.

"I remember that night. Yeah, that was a good one. Jack Daniels and excellent white powder, if I remember correctly."

Terry smiled. One of the few nights where he had sort of unburdened his troubled soul.

"Here's the thing, T," Walker said, getting out of his chair now. "All that stuff was great. It really was. But *Rolling Stone* is a magazine devoted mainly to what's happening now in pop music. Utopia and rock, man, that is the oldest of news. People don't think that way anymore."

"I know, Jim," Terry said. "But those dreams shouldn't be lost, you know? I mean why was *Stone* even founded? Not just to make money but to be the leader in the new consciousness."

He couldn't believe he had said the words "new consciousness." Jesus, nowadays it sounded like something as archaic as "23 skidoo" or "Oh, you kid."

Walker, however, nodded at him.

"Yeah, that's right. But we were kids then, Terry. I know you aren't as naive as you sound here. That shit is over with. Rock'n'roll, disco, it's all show business now. Listen. I know these guys from upstate, band called Bridge. They were really good. They played around Ithaca for years. Okay? They finally came down here and met with this hotshot producer, Georgio, who had listened to their tapes, and he said, 'Listen, you guys got some good music here, but I have one question for you.' They waited for him to lay it on them. Finally, he said, 'Would you be willing to play disco and paint yourselves blue? 'Cause that's what we fucking need. A blue disco band. We have a red band, and a white band. We need a blue band to make up an American flag super-image. You know what I mean?'"

"Yeah, I know exactly what you mean," Terry said angrily. "And that's the kind of shit I think we should attack. Do we have to kiss the ass of every disco creep who buys an ad in the paper?"

"Watch it, Terry. Is it possible you've forgotten that we don't create the music? We publicize and comment on it."

"Right, Terry said. "We comment. And if a writer thinks that disco stinks, he should be able to say that."

Jim Walker took a deep breath.

"You think we can run back the clock to the Summer of Love? It's all professional, now baby. All about making the greenbacks. And just as rock has grown up so has *Rolling Stone*. End of story. Anyway, Terry, I'm surprised at this sudden burst of belated idealism. You seem to spend all your time hanging with Thaddeus Bryant and Joey Gardello. Neither one of them strike me as peace and love guys. Especially Joey."

"Yeah, well you shouldn't lump them together, Jim. You read Thaddeus' novel. You know he's a serious writer."

Walker smiled in a serpentine manner.

"No doubt, Ter. No doubt. I just meant he knows how the game is played. You won't catch him singing 'Kumbaya' around the campfire."

Suddenly, Terry thought of something.

"You know, Jimmy, I remember a while back you told me that Joey was one of the smartest people on the planet. You thought he was going to be the next great indie director."

Walker shifted uneasily in his seat. He shot Terry a killer look.

"I never said that," he lied.

Terry knew he should leave it alone, but Walker had gotten on his nerves with his little lecture on how they should all grow up and worship success.

"No, man," Terry said. "I remember it. You were even talking about how we should all back him, kick in to help him make his films."

"You're out of your mind, Terry. You must have taken too much acid. I never said anything of the kind."

He sounded really angry now Terry nodded and let it die.

Fuck, this was going all wrong. Why did Walker suddenly hate Joey so much?

It didn't matter. He had to focus on getting a gig.

He tried to recoup fast.

"Okay, forget the think piece. But I still want to do the piece we agreed on last week. Flying out to Missoula to interview Warren Oates, Sam Peckinpah and Tom McGuane. The three of them getting wrecked, shooting up Livingstone. I just talked to Peckinpah's people last week and they're really excited."

There was a long ugly pause, then Walker looked at him and shook his head.

"I'm not sure that piece is right for you. I gotta tell you, I'm thinking about other writers."

Terry felt an electrical surge of panic shoot through him.

"What the fuck? That was my idea. You agreed I should do it just a few weeks ago."

"I don't recall agreeing to anything, Terry. And now that we are on this subject, I talked to the boss the other day and he hasn't really liked your last few pieces."

Terry felt himself losing his breath.

"Jann? Since when do you bow to Jann? You used to laugh at his ideas."

"Jann pays the bills, baby. And if he's not laughing neither am I. Or you. He told me your work is too old school. Too fucking snarky. Too anti-disco. Too ironic. You write stuff like that and we lose out access to the agency's other artists."

"The 'agency'? Who the fuck is the 'agency'?"

"The Marty Boone Publicity Agency. They control ten different artists. So if you get nasty and laugh at one of them, they fucking cut you off from interviewing all the other people they rep. That's how it is, Ter. Rock is corporate now. The happy hippy-dippy days are over. Its big money and they aren't going to let some little freelance writer stop the cash flow."

Terry had heard of this before, but somehow hadn't taken it seriously. The crew at *Stone* always laughed and jeered at the music businesspeople. They were, he'd thought, natural enemies. Once again, it appeared that he'd been dead wrong.

"So what do I have to do to continue my freelance job?"

Terry said. "Give every artist I interview a blow job?

"I wouldn't put it that way," Walker said. "But you have to learn something. We're not in the irony business, Terry. We're in the star-making business. You used to write about the rockers with real empathy, T. The last few stories have been snarky and ultra-ironic, like you were deeming to come down from your throne on high to enlighten us about their tiny achievements. To tell you the truth, I've had a lot of complaints."

Terry swallowed hard. Was this true? Was there something happening to his writing? Thaddeus had noticed the same thing in his fiction writing. Was he turning into some kind of Irony Machine?

"Well, I suppose I could tone down my work a little bit..."

Now Walker smiled at him in a totally different way. Like an animal sizing up his prey.

"There's something else too. Since you brought up Joey, there's a rumor going around that you not only buy drugs from Joey but that you sell them at your place too."

"Jim, come on. You were actually at my place one time when Joey was there. I just let him use it so the downtown gang wouldn't have to truck all the way up to the West Side. You know I'm not actually in business with him."

Walker rubbed his chin like he was having a deep thought.

"Yeah, well, that's not what I heard. And, more importantly, it's not what the boss heard either. Joey's a jerk, Terry."

"I thought you and he were tight?"

Walker looked at him in a hard way.

"No. That was never true. I put up with him because

you and Thaddeus were tight with him."

"Me? I'm only friends with him because he's Thaddeus' best friend from childhood. You know that."

Walker looked nervous again. He got up and faced the window. From his office he could see Central Park.

"Look, Terry. I just don't think I can use you for anything right now. The truth is you're a little dead around here."

Terry felt his fingertips grow cold. He didn't even have enough to pay this month's rent and now his one sure gig was gone.

"But, Jim, what did I do?"

"Just the way it is. I'll see you around sometime," Walker said. "Good luck with your great American novel. When it comes out, send me a copy. Maybe we can review it."

Terry felt a heavy pressure in his chest. Was he having a fucking heart attack?

"Jesus, Jimmy," he said.

But Jim Walker had sat back down and was looking down at his desk, fumbling with some papers, like Terry was already gone.

His stomach churning in fear and embarrassment, Terry walked down Fifth Avenue toward the Village. An unseasonably hot fall day, the sun beat down on him and he felt the sweat rolling down his arms. The streets were filled with shoppers and people bumped into him as he staggered along, feeling like he was a homeless person looking for a doorway to crash in.

Fucking Walker. He knew better. Why the hell was he

doing this to Terry? Had someone told him this story about him going into business with Joey?

Oh man. This was seriously bad.

He felt breathless, like he'd just snorted Drano instead of coke.

He had to get himself together. He had to get money, and fast. But most of the other freelancers he knew either pretended they were broke or really were. Christ, there was only one person. Thaddeus. Yeah, Thaddeus would understand. Thaddeus would probably advance him the money he needed.

But he hated asking him. Christ, he already felt like a sponge when he was with Thaddeus at Elaine's.

But still, like Thaddeus said, he had to finish his novel, get better established. Then he could leave guys like Jimmy Walker behind.

He thought of his novel. *Bad Boy.* The story of a wild and crazy freelance writer and his affairs, drug habits, hanging out in the city. Hell, there was one good thing about what had just happened in Walker's office. He could use it in his book.

On the other hand, what fucking book? He hadn't looked at it in so long, he wasn't sure if what he'd written was any good or just hip garbage.

Terry saw a phone booth, went inside and dialed. The phone rang four times, and then, a very sleepy sounding Thaddeus answered.

"Oh shit," Terry said. "Did I wake you?"

"No, well, yes, but no matter. I have meetings today. What's up?"

"Speaking of which, I just had this *terrible* meeting at *Stone.*"

"Oh shit. What happened?"

Terry sat down on the hard phone booth seat and started talking. Words rushed out of him like blood running out of a sucking wound as he told Thaddeus the whole tale of his disastrous meeting with Walker.

"So basically," he said as his tale came to a close, "I'm fucked."

There was a long pause, then Thaddeus spoke.

"Nah, you aren't. You can go over to *Playboy*. I had dinner with Hugh at the mansion when I was on my book tour. You want me to make a few calls?"

Terry hesitated.

"No, that's okay. I can call them, but I was wondering if you, well, I have my rent coming up and I'm just totally broke."

"Hey, no problem," Thaddeus said. "How much do you need?"

"Well, if there was any way I could borrow a grand, that would pretty much do it."

"Okay," Thaddeus said. "I'll be at Elaine's tomorrow night. See you then."

"Jesus," Terry said, feeling a rush of gratitude. "That's great, Thad. Thanks so much."

"No problem, Ter. See you tomorrow night. Don't throw yourself under a bus. Okay?"

"Okay," Terry said. "You'll get it back, man. Every cent."

"I know I will," Thaddeus said warmly, and hung up.

Thank God for Thaddeus. At least he had enough money to get by for now.

But, Christ, how could he have lost his *Stone* gig? Maybe Jim was right after all? Why couldn't he let go of his obsession with the 1960s? It was gone, baby, gone. But somehow he was still hung up on it, stuck in the past, where people had dreamed of a new world, new people. Not just doing your work but changing the human heart.

On the other hand, Walker was right. He wasn't as innocent as he made out. He had new dreams now, new desires for fame, glory, and riches, and fuck the past.

Jesus, he was tearing himself apart.

He'd intended to catch a taxi for the final twenty blocks or so but lost in his thoughts and zoned out by the abnormally hot winter day he just kept walking until he'd found himself back below Fourteenth Street, only a few blocks from home. He turned right on Christopher Street, and finally came to the three steps which led down to the Lion's Head. He'd sworn off going there for lunch because the food was barely passable and if he started drinking at noon he wouldn't stop until the joint closed.

But after this particular close call he needed to see a friendly face, a beautiful and sympathetic face. He was pretty sure Kathy was here, working the lunch shift. But as he entered the air-conditioned bar, he remembered what Thaddeus had said, how dismissive he'd been of Kathy and her chances of making it in show biz. He hated calling people losers, summing them up on the strength of one night of drinking with them, but what if Thaddeus was right? What would Kathy be like when her acting career petered out? Would she really become some bitter suburban mom, having affairs with one of her fellow Suburban Players like a character in a Richard Yates novel?

Was pining away for her just another fantasy of his? A

good, attractive, solid person he could count on, who maybe would understand his crazy hang-up on the dreams of the 1960s?

And now he wondered what Valerie Stevenson would say if he told her about his past, the fact that he was a hippie professor in upstate New York. She'd probably have a good laugh.

His eyes had trouble adjusting to the dark bar. On the left was the juke box which had added maybe three songs since 1955. One Beatles tune, "Michelle," one Rolling Stones classic, "Satisfaction," and for some reason one Hendrix hit, "Purple Haze," though when a customer played it almost all of the bartenders turned it down so low no one could hear it. All the other tunes were jazz from the 1940s and '50s. The most played song was Duke on "Take the A Train." The Head's heart was definitely stuck in the '40s. But that was a large part of the place's funky charm.

He pulled up a stool and took a seat at the bar...

"How's it going, Balmere," the big bartender Tommy said. He'd spent some time at Fort Holabird in the army and loved doing a comic Baltimore accent. Terry laughed and answered him back in kind: "It's so close out 'ere, hon, I thought I was gonna have a hard-tack."

Tommy gave his big friendly laugh and handed him a black and tan.

Terry sighed and sipped it and felt better already. And even better when Kathy Anderson came out of the doors leading into the kitchen. She was black-haired and hazel-eyed and her tight waitress dress accentuated her terrific figure. But more than that, there was something so alive and sweet in her eyes. He couldn't look at her without wanting to kiss her.

She carried a tray with a salad, rolls, and a lamb chop on it. She smiled and headed around the corner into the dining room, mouthing the words "Be right back" as she went.

Terry sighed heavily. He felt at home here, more so than he did anywhere else in New York. The Head had its share of celebs too, but mainly it was newspaper guys, sports writers, feature men, and the occasional actor or novelist. There was less glitz than Elaine's, and the feeling was one of hominess and wise guy humor. Most of the regulars at the bar laughed at the pretensions of the Big Celebs who hung at Elaine's. They made fun of the limos, the air kissing, and the general phoniness of the stars who frequented the place. In the past, before he had started hanging out there, Terry had laughed along with them, but now he wondered, did they only strike that attitude because they weren't able to get in? Didn't they, in their secret hearts, want to be included in the uptown party of big shots just as much as he did? Was it because they were losers, well, not exactly losers, just small people who would never be known above Fourteenth Street? He hated himself for having these traitorous thoughts. Everyone at The Head had been wonderful to him since the day he moved to New York two years ago. What was happening to him? Was he turning into the very people he had always hated? Maybe that was why he wrote about the stars he interviewed in his magazine work with a certain ironic tone. It was a way of having his cake and eating it too.

Well, he'd just have to play it the new way in his magazine work. Kiss ass. But in his novel, he could be as satirical as he wanted.

Except his agent, his agent had told him satire doesn't sell. People want heroes there too. Brilliant cops and amazing supermen. Realism was as dead as Theodore Dreiser.

Every book had to at least have the potential of becoming a blockbuster.

How the fuck could he write stuff like that? The next thing he knew he would be turning out shit like Sidney Sheldon or Arthur Hailey.

Then he remembered Thaddeus. He'd done it. He'd created a great novel that was also a page turner.

It could be done after all. But could HE do it?

He ordered a cheeseburger and found himself drinking another beer before Kathy came back. As the alcohol hit he began to feel a great air of well-being. Everything was going to work out. He had the talent. He had the connections.

His thoughts were interrupted as he saw Kathy go into the kitchen. She was a little shorter than he had remembered. Or was he just comparing her to Valerie Stevenson? Those long, tapered legs. Kathy's were shorter, somehow more working class, like the legs of the townie girls he knew in Geneva.

No, what was wrong with him? He shouldn't think that way. Kathy was great, she really was. He was kind of in love with her, wasn't he?

But who knew what love was anymore? Maybe Thaddeus was right. He was only attracted to her because she was safe, like some Catholic Baltimore girls he knew in the past. Sexy, but no match for him.

Kathy finished serving a steak dinner on the opposite side of the restaurant and walked toward him. She was smiling and warm.

"How did your pitch go at *Rolling Stone*?" she said.

"Oh, went fine. Don't have a gig yet but he said he'll call me soon."

"That's good. You'll be able to pay the rent."

Terry had to change the subject fast.

"When do you get off?" he said instead, taking her small, beautiful hand in his.

"Eight...but..."

"Fine," Terry said quickly. "I'll pick you up then and we'll go to dinner at One Fifth Avenue. Then over to the Village Vanguard to hear a little jazz. Mose Allison is there tonight."

He could use his credit card for dinner now because of his influx of cash. He'd already forgotten about *Rolling Stone*. Thaddeus was right. He'd get in at *Playboy*. The boss there, Art Kretchmer, loved his work.

Now she looked pained.

"Terry, I can't. I just can't. I feel kind of under the weather."

"Come on, Kathy. What are you saying?"

"I'm saying that I don't know if I can see you anymore."

"What?"

"Look, you're busy with your career. You call me when it suits you. That's not enough for me."

"Look, hey, that's not how it is. I've just been busy..."

"Hanging with Thaddeus Bryant, up at Elaine's. I saw your picture on Page Six of the *Post* two days ago. You're headed to another league, Terry."

"No, no way," Terry said. He tried out his casual laugh which he hoped belied the fear he felt inside. He had already alienated Wenner and now he was losing Kathy too?

He reached out and took her hand.

"Look. Kathy. Tonight we could…"

"Not tonight. I'm tired and I want to go crash."

"Fine. Tomorrow night then. Kathy, I'm crazy about you."

"So you say."

"I do say it. Tomorrow night then. Let me show you."

She stopped and looked at him and there was such yearning in her eyes. Yet he could sense her distrust.

She smiled and let out a long breath.

"Oh God, Terry Brennan," she said. "What am I going to do with you?"

"You're going to give me a second chance. I'm going to take you to a great restaurant and things are going to be different. From now on. I'll pick you up at your place tomorrow at seven."

"Not at my place. I'm having painters in."

"Well, maybe we could meet at Jimmy Day's then?"

"No good. The bartender, Flanagan, hits on me every time I go in there."

"Where then?"

"I have an idea. Why don't we meet at your place. You could just give me the key and I'll go there and wait for you."

Terry felt a little strange about it. But it wouldn't be the first time she'd waited for him at his apartment.

"Terry, I'm not asking you to marry me. It would just be comfortable, that's all. Plus, I could go through all your things and find the coke you're dealing with Joey Gardello."

Terry felt a little shot of panic. Then he recalled that Kathy had been there the night Joey had dealt coke from his pad. And she hadn't liked it either.

"You know I wasn't dealing. I was just helping Joey out."

"A bad idea," Kathy said. She smiled at him in a mocking way. "So are we on?"

"Yeah. Fine," he heard himself say. "I'll leave my extra key with Abraham, the super. He lives in the building next to mine. I'll be back by seven."

Kathy laughed and smiled at him in a mischievous way.

"Sometimes, Terry, it occurs to me that I don't know you at all. Who knows what kind of trouble you could get me in?"

Terry leaned over and kissed her cheek. He was about to do it again, when Tommy's voice broke them up.

"Hey," Tommy said, giving them a stern look. "You two! This ain't a penthouse at the Pierre. We got customers in the dining room, Kathy."

Kathy laughed and kissed Terry on the cheek. Then turned and walked away, giving her ass an extra little twitch for him.

CHAPTER SIX

Grahame Court was at 118th Street and Seventh Avenue. Sometimes called the Black Dakota, after the famous celeb building at West 72nd Street and Central Park West, the Grahame featured outlandishly gigantic apartments once owned by the black aristocracy of Harlem. The place fell into disrepair in the 1950s but was then bought by developers and restored and refurbished even beyond its original outrageous high style. In this great monster of a building lived Nicky Baines, Harlem's premier drug dealer and "forty percent legit" businessman. Nicky liked to mention the figure whenever possible, claiming he became three to five percent more legit each year, just like his heroes and role models, John D. Rockefeller and Joe Kennedy. Included in Nicky's palatial co-op was a bowling alley and a screening room with seats made of maroon velvet and gold-plated arm rests. His apartment had thirteen rooms, including an observatory on the rooftop and a special Olympic-sized swimming pool in which he held his own Summer Olympics, paying beautiful hookers huge cash prizes if they would swim naked in relay races, on which he and his drug cronies bet ridiculous sums. Which was just fine, because being the biggest coke and heroin dealer in New York City, Nicky made ridiculous sums.

Nicky lived like a king, but anyone who put a crimp in his extravagant lifestyle received harsh treatment in the extreme.

On every Monday, Nicky held his own private court with himself as prosecutor, judge, and jury. There was no public defender in this court room.

In what he called his Throne Room, Nicky sat on an actual throne one of his Italian drug buddies had stolen for him from one of Lucrezia Borgia's minor castles. Nicky wore a five-thousand-dollar custom-made suit, a big Power Yellow tie with pictures of Lena Horne at age twenty-one painted on it and two-thousand-dollar designer shoes made of peccary.

In front of him now stood a beaten young black man with blood running down his neck. His name was Alexander and he handled all of Nicky's security. For his efforts Alexander was paid the princely sum of 500,000 dollars a year. Next to Alexander were two other black men, each of them chiseled, powerful, their faces tense, their eyes blank, as though they were robotic sentries waiting to be plugged into action. Their names were Bo and Earle and they were Nicky's private guards.

"That's right," Nicky said now. "Five hundred thousand bucks a year and all I ask you to do is to keep your eye on any miscreants who might want to waltz off with what is rightly mine. You have any means at your disposal, any weapons, more tech gadgets than James Bond, any number of trained men for your own private division. For that matter, any women you want. Anything your soulful heart desires, Alexander, and yet you allowed someone, and we think we know who, to skip away with three hundred thousand dollars in cocaine and four hundred thousand dollars in cash. Right out of one of our armored trucks."

Alexander tried very hard not to shake as he spoke.

"You realize, sir, that two of the suspects are dead. Joey Gardello and his brother Ray."

"Yes, I do realize that. I also realize that the cocaine and the money have not been retrieved. And that you seem no closer to retrieving them that you were at this time yesterday."

"That's not quite true, "Alexander said. "We are looking hard at several other suspects."

Now Alexander felt a great desire to relieve himself down his own leg.

Suddenly, the mercurial Nicky smiled in his warm fatherly way, and his voice became oh so kind.

"I believe you, Alexander," Nicky said. "But don't let me down again. It has come to my attention that one of the people we must interview is a Mr. Willie Hudson. Are we in agreement on this?"

"Yes, sir," Alexander said. "Also a second suspect, who lives in the Village and who used his apartment as a sort of downtown office for Gardello's business. A hotshot journalist name of Terry Brennan."

"I want both their asses in here as soon as possible," Nicky said. "Is that understood, Alex?"

"Yes, it is. Of course," said Alexander. "I have my men searching for them, even as we speak."

"Even as we speak," Nicky said. "I do like that. It reminds me of George Saunders films. I always liked the way he spoke, don't you?"

"Yes, of course," Alex said.

Though Alexander had had this particular bit of conversation with Nicky many times before, he managed to nod in a childlike and excitable way, as if he was hearing

Nicky's classy reference for the first time.

Nicky had some kind of strange brain disorder which caused him to obsess on words and phrases he picked up from movies, television and real life. If they were words and phrases which pleased him, he often became gentle and understanding. If they weren't...well, it was better not to think about what happened if they weren't.

"I am confident you will come back home by the end of the week with Hudson and Brennan and everything they have taken from me. Do you understand?"

"Yes, sir," Alexander said. "Got it."

"Good," Nicky said. "Don't fail me, Alexander. One week. If you are ever caught asleep at the wheel again, you're through. Done. Next case."

Alexander nodded and tried to stop his knees from shaking.

The two goons half-carried him out of the Throne Room and led him to a gold-paneled elevator, barely big enough for two people. Nicky Baines liked it because it was New York's smallest elevator. The reason he knew it was New York's smallest elevator was because there was a gold plaque screwed into the teakwood elevator walls which said, "World's Smallest Elevator." Nicky had paid five thousand dollars to a drugged-out sculptor to design the plaque. He touched it reverently each time he entered the small chamber.

"One week," one of Nicky's goons, Bo, said.

Then they threw him inside and hit the DOWN button. Alexander slumped against the wall and wept with relief and terror, knowing that even as bad as it had been, he was still a very lucky man. The last man who had failed Nicky had been taken to a body shop and had an electric drill inserted into his anus.

As the elevator went down, Alexander told himself to stop shaking, to get himself together now and find Willie Hudson and that journalist, Terry Brennan.

He came down to the underground parking garage and quickly headed to his steel-plated Mercedes. He was still shaking inside but he didn't have time now to be afraid. If he wanted to stay alive, he had to move. And fast.

CHAPTER SEVEN

Terry hustled back to his apartment and looked at *Bad Boy*. There was some wild stuff in there. His crazy adventure saving suicidal Howard Freeman from jumping off the roof. Another time with his agent Barry Landsman out in Hollywood, when the two of them had come up with a movie idea about helicopter tree rustling while waiting to see a producer and sold it in five minutes for fifty grand. Where had all that money gone? Into snorting coke, eating at Elaine's, and too many good times.

Yeah, there was a lot of great material here, wonderful stuff, but as the booze wore off, he saw the novel in a clear way. It was a pile of anecdotes, the kind of stuff that really played at the bar, or, for that matter, in the editor's office when he was pitching a magazine piece—New York editors loved to hear crazy Hollywood stories. But if it was going to be a novel then there had to be a spine, a plot, something that would carry the reader all the way through. Something about...about...about who knew the fuck what?

The Moral Growth of a Bad Boy through pain and suffering. Yeah, that was it. The hero, Ryan Matthews, had to be an innocent who comes to New York full of hopes and dreams but meets all kinds of sharp people who con him, bamboozle him, and not only men but women, too.

Women who are beautiful and decadent and alluring, women whom he fucks and falls for and who use him badly. But he can't be just an innocent. He has to learn from these oh-so-alluring people and soon he is as bad as the rest of them, cheating, lying, and hustling his way through the city but then...then...

Then he put the novel down, went into his closet and started ransacking his way through old drafts of abandoned stories, outlines for screenplays, yet unwritten.

And there, in the back, in a gray manuscript box was his Baltimore novel, about his old buddies at the steel plant. Guys he had grown up with, sweated with, while working on the slag heap. Guys who were funny and wild in their own way. Guys who would never want to sit in the Bridge and Tunnel Bar. But would rather get hammered at Joe's All-American Bar in South Baltimore.

The book was called *Steel* and he'd written about a hundred pages of it before he'd shown it around and gotten such a negative response. What was the point of going on?

He brought it to his desk and opened it up and began to read. A scene where a guy gets fired from his job and goes on a bender, ends up with a hooker.

He read it over slowly and all he could think is "This is good stuff. Maybe. Maybe I could still..."

But he never completed the thought. He was too tired, exhausted from the fear he'd felt pulling him down deeper and deeper into depression.

What if they wouldn't hire him anymore?

What would happen to him?

He couldn't bear to go back to teaching. And they might not even want him back. He'd walked out, and though he'd try to do it in a nice way, he knew some of his fellow professors hated him for leaving. They wouldn't forget. He'd left them and by his action he'd branded them cowards.

What would he do…?

The question remained unanswered as he fell asleep with his head on his desk.

Eight hours later, there was some insistent sound, pulling him out of his slumber.

The telephone. He looked at it, then out the window. It was dark. How long had he slept?

He picked it up.

"Hello?"

"Hey, Terry. Where the hell have you been? I called ten times and left two messages with your service."

"Thaddeus, hello. I'm sorry. Didn't check my service."

"Then you haven't heard."

"Heard what?"

"Joey…Joey Gardello is dead."

"What? You joking?"

"No joke, Ter. They found him in Central Park, under a walkover. Somebody shot him a couple of times. His brother, Ray, too."

"Oh, man," Terry said. "They have any idea who did it?"

"Drugs. Somehow it's connected to drugs. He was out there late at night. I've already talked to Rosalie. She thinks he may have been working for Nicky Baines. They'd had some argument and maybe Joey felt like Nicky had shorted him on a deal. She thinks it's possible he robbed one of Nicky's trucks to get even."

Now Terry was wide awake.

"Robbing Nicky Baines? Talk about a fucking death wish."

"I know, but I can see it," Thaddeus said. "That's how Joe was. If you dissed him, he'd come back full bore."

"How much money is he alleged to have robbed?"

"Not sure. But plenty."

"So where is the money?" Terry said. Though the whole thing was tragic the reporter in him had already taken over.

"You and Nicky Baines want to know. And the cops."

"Wow," Terry said. "Any chance Rosalie knows and isn't saying?"

"Nah, she'd never be involved. Why don't you ask her at the funeral?"

"What?"

"That's why I called. I have to go up there and wish you'd come with me. It's tough facing the old neighborhood alone. Besides, you knew Joey too. I know you guys had a few words, but he told me many times how much he respected your work. He really thought you'd write a great book someday."

"Sure. Of course I'll come."

"Okay. Thursday at one. I'll meet you at the funeral home. One p.m. You got a pen?"

"Let me look here a minute."

"Hey, and don't worry. I'll have your money with me."

Terry felt a sharp tremor of guilt.

"Oh sure, thanks." Like it was an afterthought, like his whole life didn't depend on that money.

He scrambled through papers and dead bottles on his desk. Finally found a Bic. Wrote down the funeral home address.

"Thanks, Thad. It means a lot to me."

"Of course," Thaddeus said.

After hanging up, Terry thought of the two (or was it three?) times he'd let Joey deal from his pad. He thought of Kathy. Jesus, what would she make of this? Could the cops somehow get his name? Nah, that was ridiculous.

He'd go to the funeral, come back, and he and Kathy could talk it all out.

He was going to be fine.

But poor Joey and his good, kind brother Ray. What the hell had they gotten involved in?

CHAPTER EIGHT

The Timmons Funeral Home was a hideous place with green walls and worn carpets. The cheap casket was small comfort for the stiff inside. Joey had been made up hideously, his lips puffed up like a blowfish. His eyes weren't right either, or his cheeks were inflated like he was lying there with nuts stuffed into his jaws. A dead blowfish/squirrel.

Thaddeus looked down at him and Terry saw his knees buckle.

He began to weep.

A black-haired woman in a black dress and a black lace shawl over her head came toward them.

"Thaddeus," she said. "Let me get you something to drink."

She nodded at Terry and he realized that he'd met her before. Rosalie Torres, Joey's ex-wife. She was hollow-eyed, had obviously been crying, but she looked strong, stronger than either of them.

They walked to a smaller, side room and sat down. She handed Thaddeus a flask from her purse.

He looked up at her and managed a smile.

"Joey's flask," he said.

"Yeah, I figured it was probably the last time I'd ever use it."

"Okay," Thaddeus said quietly, and took a long pull.

He handed it to Terry who did likewise. Hot Jack Daniels burned his throat.

"What about Ray?"

"His funeral is tomorrow. His wife and kids didn't want to bury them together."

Rosalie looked around at the flowers, which seemed to already be drooping.

"Flowers," she said. "So many. I used to think it was so we'd think of life instead of death, but I heard from the undertaker last night. The real reason they have all the flowers is to hide the scent of all the chemicals inside the corpse. Without the flowers the room would smell like a science project."

"Joey would love that," Thaddeus said. And kissed Rosalie's cheek.

Terry and Thaddeus stood in the small gathering at the funeral. The priest, Father Torelli, spoke a few words about what a brilliant guy and loving friend Joey was. The other guests, aunts and uncles, stood silently, one man looking nervously at his watch.

The pallbearers, including Thaddeus, carried Joey's coffin from the hearse to the grave. Rain began to fall, a light rain, though, and Terry thought there was something poetic about it, something theatrical which Joey might appreciate. People took out their umbrellas and waited as Thaddeus stepped up to a microphone by the head of the grave. He tapped the mike a couple of times and sadly shook his head.

"What is a friend? Aristotle said it best, I think. 'A friend is a single soul dwelling in two bodies.' At least that's a description of Joey and myself. As kids we were inseparable. We ran these streets, the beloved and fearful streets of our neighborhood, The Bronx, together, playing our children's games, sometimes swiping apples or a candy bar. We read comic books together. We went to the old Zenith Theatre, and that's where Joey fell in love with the movies. Soon, Joey was movie crazy. At age twelve, Joey's Uncle Vincent gave him his first eight-millimeter camera. I can still see Joe now running around with it, making his films of everyday life. He would interview me and all of our pals until it drove us crazy. If we got a hit in pick-up baseball, he'd be there with the camera in our faces asking us what it felt like. It made us all feel like Mickey Mantle or Willie Mays. But as we got older, he graduated to tougher questions. 'I saw you looking at Judy Alter down the block. Do you like Judy? What do you feel like when she wears those short shorts, the white ones that are too tight?' Soon he was making his own documentary shorts films, bugging Uncle Vincent to give him enough money to put it all together as a full-length documentary. He was amazing. He'd read what I wrote in my black and white notebook and then he'd say, 'One day we're going to film one of your books...' And I'd say, 'I don't know if I'll ever write one.' But Joey was sure I would. He believed in me."

"I carried that belief with me to Vietnam and remembering Joey and our friendship helped me get through. It was funny, though. Joey was always the tougher of us, but he didn't pass the physical for 'Nam. Joe and his flat feet. When I got back, I was pretty lost for a while, hitching around to California, falling in love with a hippie girl. I thought I'd found something, but the so-called nonjudgmental hippies didn't like vets. When we had a vet parade in San Francisco people actually spit on us. So much for the hippie brotherhood. I came back to New York, lost and maybe feeling a little sorry for myself. But Joey wouldn't hear any of that. It was he who kept me afloat. No matter how down he was, he always had time for his old friend."

Thaddeus stumbled, struggled to keep going.

"Now, Joey Gardello is gone. But, I'll always keep him in my heart and soul. Where Joe really lives now is inside all of us who loved him, and we'll never forget him. Goodbye Joey. My brother. My friend."

Terry found tears dripping down his face. He squeezed Thaddeus' arm as he stepped back from the grave.

As they drove across town, Terry had to ask again.

"You really think Nicky Baines is looking for the money?"

"Wouldn't you?"

"You mean if I was a drug running murderous bastard? Yeah, I guess so. There's just something wrong with that, though."

"What?"

"Why would he shoot them in the park? Wouldn't he want to torture them first, get them to give up the dough, then kill them?"

Thaddeus nodded.

"That makes sense. But Joey always had a piece with him. So did Ray. They probably resisted, and they had to off them there."

"Yeah," Terry said. "Or they could have already found the money and killed them afterwards."

"Yeah. That's right."

"Yeah, of course. Well, maybe it had nothing to do with Nicky. It wasn't like he was Joey's only enemy. Or the only one looking for the money."

"What do you mean?"

"I don't know. I'm just spitballing. But if Joey did rob a truck, he'd need help. More than Ray. Guys to somehow stop the truck, guys who told him when the truck was coming. Guys to deal with the guards in the back of the truck. Now say Joey gets the money, and he's decided to rip off the other guys in his crew. See how it might go. They might have gotten the money and decided to off Joey and Ray so they couldn't come back on them."

"Fuck. I hadn't thought of that."

Thaddeus shook his head.

"Fucking Joey. He had a lot of guts. But thinking about the consequences of his acts? That was another story. We used to call him Captain Impulsive. You can almost make book that was his downfall."

As they rolled along in the mist Terry felt moody and strangely exhausted by the whole morning and afternoon. Then as they approached Third Avenue he remembered his date with Kathy. He couldn't be late again. And if he headed off to Elaine's with Thaddeus it could easily become an instant replay of the other night.

"Look, Thaddeus. I have to go home."

"You don't want to go get a drink?"

"Nah. I'm wasted. This whole thing was exhausting."

"Well, thanks for coming, Terry."

Thaddeus reached into his jacket and pulled out an envelope stuffed with cash.

"Here you go. I almost forgot."

"Thanks, Thaddeus. And you know I'll pay you as soon as I sell my next piece."

"Don't worry about that, pal," Thaddeus said. "You really helped me today. I won't ever forget it."

CHAPTER NINE

Detective Maury Lazenby punched Willie Hudson in the head, sending him sprawling across the interrogation room. Willie felt he was going to puke. Then he noticed the puke green color of the walls. He wondered if they had been painted that color to induce you to puke. If so it was working.

"You can beat me all you want, Officer, but I don't know nothing about Joey Gardello's drug business. Him and me was friends, is all."

"Yeah, good friends who sold drugs and stole drugs. Look, we know what kind of guy Joey was. And we know what kind of guy you are. You work as a bouncer at Studio 54. Gee, that means you have almost no contact with drugs at all."

"I see drugs there, sure, but I don't sell 'em."

"Right," Green said. "When people ask you if you're holding you say, 'No fucking way. I am not in any way involved with drugs.' Right."

"Where were you the other night at two in the morning?" Lazenby said.

"At my job. Man, we don't even get started till one in the morning. I was right there and I can get me about fifty witnesses to back me up, you dig?"

"How nice for you, Willie."

Willie sat back down in the chair. His mouth was bleeding. His head ached. The walls were still puke green. He looked at the tape recorder which was rolling in front of Lazenby.

"We wonder if maybe you slipped out for a while, ran back up to the West Side and wasted Joey and Ray Gardello, then came back down to the big disco party?"

"No, man, I didn't. I didn't do nothing like that at all."

"Maybe you helped him steal some drugs and then stole them for yourself. Maybe his brother and him were going to come after you and you hit them first?"

"And maybe there is fucking unicorns in Central Park too, Officers. But you can't prove it if they don't exist."

Hesitantly, Willie got up out of his chair. His stomach seemed to fall somewhere below his knees but he got up.

"Before you go, Willie, we got one final little question for you. What do you know about this guy Terry Brennan?"

Willie stopped cold. Terry Brennan? The guy who had the Village pad?

He didn't want to involve Terry Brennan in any of this, but, on the other hand, it might do him some good to give the cops something. Keep them off his back.

"Yeah, Brennan, I know him. He was a friend of Joey's. Joey used his pad in the Village to deal coke sometimes."

"Hmmm," Lazenby said. "You think he's a player?"

"I don't know for sure," Willie said. "But he's one of those *Rolling Stone* journalists. You know how it is. Those guys are all crazy."

The two cops looked at one another and smiled.

"You happen to have Mr. Brennan's address?"

"Don't know the number, but it's on the corner of

Barrow and Hudson in the West Village."

Green wrote down the address on his note pad.

"Thank you, Willie. Have a most pleasant day," Lazenby said. "We'll be meeting with you again soon, so don't go on vacation."

"Shit," Willie said. "You need money to vacate. Money like those drug dealers have."

Willie walked out of the interrogation room. It sucked getting beat up on, but he came out okay. Though he did feel a little bad about involving that guy Brennan. Seemed like a good dude.

Then again, he was some kind of drug dealer. What the hell? Maybe he did off Joey and Ray.

CHAPTER TEN

Terry walked down Barrow Street, watching a young teacher herding a class of fourth graders along the block. Members of the Village Community School. They were all cute and suddenly he had this image of himself and Kathy with their own two brats, whizzing along on the curving Village streets on skateboards.

A boy and a girl. The happiest family in existence.

So unlike the miserable, mind-dragging home he'd grown up in. With insane scream-outs every night. His father walking around the house in his Navy shorts screaming at both Terry and his mother about what losers they were.

No wonder he wanted to be a star. A star didn't have to feel that kind of pain. A star was beyond such mundane misery.

Of course, he knew that wasn't true. But having money and fame meant you were loved everywhere you went. Look at Mick! Mick didn't have to worry about where his next check would come from. No one talked to Mick like Jim Walker had talked to him. Mick would snap his fingers and Jim Walker would fucking disappear!

Maybe he had been looking at all of this the wrong way.

He *could* have it all…Kathy and family and literary stardom…and…and…

And what the hell was that just down the street?

Oh man. This was definitely not part of the dream. Nonono. Two cop cars parked right by his place at 72 Barrow. Three or four cops wandering around, and one of them seemed to be coming out of the side entrance which went into the storage bins below the apartments. It was there people had their own cubicles and could store old furniture, beds, things maybe they still wanted in case they moved to a bigger place but weren't using now. What were the cops doing there?

Of course, he told himself, as he stumbled on, suddenly alert, of course this has nothing to do with me. They were there because one of the neighbors got drunk and smacked his wife around or maybe the crazy street vet Shorty had flipped out again.

The only problem was that two cops were walking toward him now. Plain clothes cops, but cops for sure. You could tell by the way they nosed around, like they were sniffing the bricks in his building. And the taller, black cop was holding a shoe box of some kind.

"Hey, you there?" said the white guy. "You happen to be Terry Brennan?"

Terry flinched as if hit by a bullet. He wanted to say "Yeah, I'm him, what of it?" like some kind of movie tough guy, but the words wouldn't come out. He looked to his right and saw the wooden door to Chumley's. Rather, a door which led to the little garden just outside the bar, a place called Pamela's Court. He stared at the two cops who walked briskly toward him. Felt creeping panic in his arms and legs.

"I'm Detective Lazenby. You Brennan? 'Cause we need to talk to you about something," the trim, white detective said.

"I'm not him," Terry improvised. "I know him though. He lives down on Grove I think."

"Is that right?" the black cop said. They were a few feet away from him now.

"You look exactly like the picture we have of him," the black cop said.

"What picture?"

"The one that was in *Rolling Stone Magazine* last month."

He pulled out a picture taken of Terry as he hobnobbed with fellow journalist Lucian Truscott at a party at Elaine's.

"All right," Terry said. "What is it you guys want?"

"Just like to know where you got this," the black cop said.

He held up the Nike shoebox and opened it. Terry looked inside and felt his heart skip beats. The box was filled with white powder. Cocaine.

"I don't know anything about that," Terry said.

"No?" the white cop said. "Then how come we found it in your storage locker beneath your apartment five minutes ago? That and twenty thousand bucks in cash."

Terry felt a stab of fear in his gut but anger as well.

"Maybe you guys put it there," he said.

"No, sir," Green said. "We think perhaps you put it there after robbing it from your friend, Joey Gardello."

"I think not," Terry said.

Holy shit. This wasn't happening. This was right out of the *Twilight Zone*.

"No idea, huh?" Green said.

He reached for his handcuffs and then Terry did something he would have never imagined himself capable of.

He pushed the black cop into the white cop and somehow they tripped over one another, both of them tumbling into the gutter. The box of cocaine fell from the black cop's hand and flew out into the street, the coke sailing away on a helpful breeze.

Without thinking what he would do next, Terry found himself opening the door to Chumley's courtyard. Once inside, he ducked into the bar itself where six or seven people were still drinking. He ran down the length of the bar, then came to the second door.

He counted on the cops not knowing that Chumley's was an old speakeasy and that its owner Leland Stanford Chumley had run liquor from the place. Old Leland had purposely left both the Barrow and Bedford Street entrances unmarked. So Terry could escape on Bedford.

He opened the old Escape Hatch (as the regulars called it) and looked out on the street. Neither of the cops were there. Then he was outside and racing down the street. At Grove he took a left and ran to Hudson, where a taxicab was rumbling uptown.

He got in, slammed the door and told the driver to take him to Fourteenth Street.

Back inside Chumley's, Lazenby and Green looked at all the booths, in the men's room and then asked the ancient bartender, Rafe, if he'd seen a guy come in running.

Rafe looked at them quizzically.

"When would this be?"

"When? Like now," Lazenby said.

"Now? You mean *just* now? Or in the past? And if it is the past would it be the semi-distant past, or would it be like the more immediate recent past?"

The two cops looked at one another.

"You know what, man," Green said, "It would be a few seconds ago, and if you are hiding him in a broom closet or something your ass could soon be sitting in a cell as an accessory."

Rafe dried a glass with a greasy towel and smiled.

"Accessory to what? Cocaine smuggling?"

"How did you happen to know that?" Lazenby asked.

"Yeah," Green said. "Brennan happen to come in here dealing his product?"

Rafe smiled and flashed them a gold tooth with a star engraved in it.

"Not at all," he said. "I just guessed it. See, you have the terrible white medication all over your suit, officer."

He nodded to Green, who looked down at his coke-dusted sport coat.

"You might want to have that pressed before you get back to your precinct," Rafe said.

"You're funny," Green said. "Maybe you won't be so amusing when we come down and roust this place."

Unfazed, Rafe turned toward the tap and poured a customer a beer.

Green and Lazenby turned to walk out the way they'd come in. Then Lazenby noticed the Bedford Street door.

"So, he went out here?" he said to Rafe. "That it?"

"Is that what?" Rafe said. "I do not understand what 'it' refers to. But then I'm from Antigua and English is my second language, Officer."

He turned away to deliver the beer to a village antique dealer.

Lazenby swore under his breath, as Green tried to knock the coke off of his shirt.

"Any of you other guys see anyone coming through here?"

Silence.

"The fucking Village," Green said. "The whole place is run by goddamned pirates."

Then they hurried out the old Escape Hatch only to face an empty street.

CHAPTER ELEVEN

The sun was almost down when Terry hit Howard's buzzer hard. He could hear it squawking upstairs. But no one came. Shit, maybe Howard had picked up some girl last night and ended up at her place.

But suddenly, thankfully, the window opened above him and a frizzy-haired, lizard-eyed Howard leaned out.

"Terry, what are you doing down there, man?"

"Howard, let me in. It's serious."

"Okay, man."

He buzzed the door and Terry staggered up the steps.

Howard's living room was a wreck. Papers and magazines tossed all over the floor and on his battered chairs–all two of them. His couch was missing a leg and was propped up with a couple of bricks which made it lopsided. When Terry sat down, he immediately started falling to the left and began to feel he was in some German Expressionist movie.

Howard went into the kitchen and came out with two cans of Rolling Rock beer.

Terry took a large sip, but the stuff was warm, putrid.

"Where's my birthday present?" Howard said, with a twinkle in his eye.

"Sorry. I'll get it for you later. This is serious, Howie."

"I was just kidding about the present. What the hell's going on?" Howard said. "You look like a run over duck."

"Worse than that. The cops are after me."

"The cops? For what?" Howard sounded astounded and almost hysterical, his favorite mode of being.

"For, you won't believe this, for stealing cocaine."

"Jesus, what happened? You sell a gram to some under-cover cop or something?"

Terry slid down the couch and propped himself up as he spoke.

"No! I said 'stealing' not 'dealing.' For Chrissakes, Howie, you know I don't deal coke."

Howard walked around in a circle and ran his hands through his frizzy, prematurely white hair.

"Well, I didn't think you did. But, then again, you sold me some at your place a couple of months ago. I'd call that dealing. I bet the cops would too."

Terry said nothing. God, had Howard been there that night? He had been so ashamed of it that he had tried to forget who actually was there. Now it rushed back to him. Howard, Gina Wade, Joey and Joey's friend, the black dude who worked as a bouncer at Studio 54, Willie Hudson. They were all getting stoned and felt great about it, but now it had turned around on him. Somehow his whole reputation was ruined by the few times he'd let Joey deal from his place.

Howard looked down at him with this prosecutor's stare.

"Come off of it, Howard. I noticed that you didn't mind it when you were getting wasted over at my place."

"Hey," Howard said, "I'm not getting all moral on you, but I'm just saying…you did sell coke there."

"I didn't. Joey did. You know that. It's not like I have it

sitting around. But they found it in my storage locker with twenty grand."

Howard started laughing in a mocking way.

"Jesus, Terry, why'd you stash it there? Isn't that kind of obvious?"

Terry stood up and shouted in Howard's face.

"Did you fucking hear a word I said? I didn't stash it anywhere. It's not my money and it's not my coke."

"Whatever you say. Listen, Terry, how'd you think to come here?"

"I had to get off the street. Christ, Howard."

"But how'd you get away from the cops?"

Terry explained how he'd pushed the cops into one another and made his getaway through Chumley's.

"Oh man. You punched a cop?" Howard said. "That's gonna be another charge against you, Ter. First dealing. Then, assaulting a police officer. Holy shit. You're like the hipster John Dillinger."

Terry couldn't stand it any longer. He grabbed Howard by the collar and shook him.

"I did not 'assault' anybody. It was more like a nudge and they got all twisted up and they both fell off the curb. It was just a reflexive thing, Howard. You know I don't assault people."

Howard looked down at his throat, where Terry's hand clutched tighter.

"Sorry, but you're kind of assaulting me right now, Ter. If you see what I mean."

Terry let go and smoothed out Howard's shirt.

"Sorry," he said. "But calling it assault, Jesus, Howard."

"Okay, it wasn't really 'assault'," Howard said. "But wait till the cops tell the judge. They'll say you kicked one of them in the balls and head-butted the second one. What are you going to do?"

"I have to find out who set me up. Who and why they did it."

Howard nodded and walked into the kitchen. Terry followed him in and wished he hadn't. There was a pile of dishes in the sink with white and green ooze on them. There was an old pizza on the Bakelite table and some empty bottles of Robutussin AC lying in the sink. The smell was primordial.

"Sorry about the odor. You want a sandwich?"

He opened the fridge and the odor of rotted liverwurst smothered the room.

"Guess the liverwurst is about the 'wurst' it's ever been," Howard said, giving a nervous little laugh.

"Jesus," Terry said.

Terry went back into the other room, trying to keep himself from puking. Howard traipsed in after him.

There was an ancient easy chair, with one of its arms ripped open to reveal an orange spongy interior, which Howard had half taped up with prison-gray duct tape.

Terry found a yellow legal pad on the seat of the chair, picked it up and started to put it aside so he could sit down. Then he glanced at it. On the top were the words "Oates and Peckinpah Piece for *Stone*."

"What the fuck is this, Howard?"

"What's what?"

"This looks like notes you're making for my fucking piece for *Stone*."

"No. I mean…Well, Jimmy Walker said you were off of it. So, you know, he like put me on it."

"I just talked to Jim about this," Terry said. "And you

knew this was my piece."

"No way. Well, I was going to mention it but then I thought I should check with Walker first. He said you didn't want to write for them anymore. Now that you're finishing your novel."

Terry felt himself exploding inside.

"It was you. You were the one who told Walker I was dealing from my apartment."

There was the briefest of guilty pauses before Howard spoke.

"No. C'mon, Terry. It wasn't me."

But Howard's cheeks were turning red.

"You did it, you fuck," Terry said. "So you could get my story. You came over and got wasted and then told Walker I was a drug dealer."

He moved toward Howard, who picked up his battered old Harmony guitar.

"Fuck you, Terry. You're out of your mind. Dealing coke and punching cops. And now accusing me of ruining your career. You need help man. Maybe you should check into Bellevue, asshole."

"You son of a bitch. This was my gig!"

"Hey," Howard said, holding the guitar like a shield. "It isn't like you can just fly out there and hang out with them. You're a wanted man, Brennan."

Howard was smiling when he said it.

Terry heard the mockery in his voice. Had he just made up the fact that Howard was this loyal old hippie pal? Had he needed a fellow writer to trust so he invented "loyalty" as Howard's great attribute?

Wasn't he just another slimeball hustling his way to the top, willing to step on anyone and everyone who got in his way? For that matter, Terry thought, wasn't he himself exactly the same as Howard? He didn't want to believe so, but maybe it was true.

"Look at you," Howard said. "You think I'm the bad guy here. But it was you who blew off my birthday to hang out with your bigshot friend Thaddeus Bryant. It's you who doesn't answer my calls anymore. Who's frozen me out of the holy inner circle of Thaddeus and Joey, and Gina Wade. Letting Joey use your place to deal coke? You think he's cool? He's not, man. He's a scumbag. And he's your good pal. Think about it, pal. You're the one who's changed, Terry. You're not a friend anymore, not really. You're just another player."

Terry felt as though his head would explode. He moved toward Howard, who swung the guitar at him. Terry ducked under it and came up with a punch in Howard's gut. Howard fell on the floor, wheezing. Terry felt horrible. Hitting his old friend. He tried to kneel down to see if Howard was okay, but Howard had gotten his breath back and was screaming at him.

"Fuck you, Brennan. You asshole. You think you're better than me. You pretend you're a nice guy but you're the one who is a shit. I'm glad I took your gig. Your great novel. That's all bullshit. You have five seconds to get out of here before I call the cops."

"Look, I'm sorry, man. But what you did…"

But friendly, cuddly, Koren-like Howard's face was now twisted into a kind of devil's grimace. His voice was high and tortured, like a man being burned alive.

"Fuck you. I hate you, you son of a bitch. You think you're so fucking cool. Hanging with Thaddeus all the time. Never have time for your old pals anymore. Writing your big novel. I can't wait until they pick you up, you shithead. Those cops will fuck you up the ass until your fucking hemorrhoids flame out. Now get out of here. Asshole!"

Terry headed down the steps, hearing Howard's demonic screams all the way to the front door.

"Don't come back here again, Terry. I'll kill you. I will."

CHAPTER TWELVE

On Eighth Avenue the sun had died and the light was watery and gray. The grimness of it all seemed to leak inside him. What did Howard mean about Joey being a scumbag? It was obvious he wasn't the straightest guy in the world, but they all liked having him around when they wanted to get stoned. Howard sounded like he was talking about more than just a little coke dealing. Maybe Joey was into far deeper shit. Which meant that the cops might think that he himself was into far deeper shit too.

Terry rubbed his throbbing forehead and walked back downtown, knowing that he was going in the wrong direction. But what was the right direction? He looked at normal people, shopping, heading off to work, going to the doctor, taking their kids to school, all the little boring things that Terry always found a drag. He lived for exciting moments, interviews, hanging out at Elaine's, at the Head, seeing his name in print. But now he longed for a respite from excitement. God, if he could just be anonymous and bored.

The cops hadn't seen him yet, but they would.

He longed to call Thaddeus, go up town to his place. But as soon as he had the thought he realized that the cops were already there. How many times had he been photographed with Thaddeus in the past year? At book parties, at Elaine's, at Raoul's. They were like Batman and Robin but, unfortunately, without the masks.

Suddenly, he remembered Kathy. Christ, she had been waiting at his place for close to an hour. He should call her, tell her he was late. But what if the cops were there? Waiting with her, listening in?

No, not "what if?" They were there all right, and they'd told Kathy everything to win her over to their side. How hard would that be? She'd already been suspicious of him because of him allowing Joey to use his pad to deal coke. Now they had found both coke and money in his locker. Who knew what she might think?

She might never want to see him again.

He felt dizzy, almost as though he was going to black out.

He took deep breaths, tried to clear his head.

But then he another startling thought. He wasn't being set up for dope dealing alone. He was being set up for murder. Of course. How slow could he be? He knew exactly what they must think. He and Joey had robbed Nicky, and then he had gotten greedy and robbed and killed Joey and his brother for the rest of the dope and the cash.

Which meant Nicky probably had guys out looking for him too.

He wandered on down the darkening Village streets. He was trapped now. But why? Why did someone pick him? It made no sense.

Just then he saw a car out of the corner of his eye, rolling behind him. At first he thought he was just being paranoid, but now he was sure.

He turned, faced it. Christ, there it was, a huge black limo just behind him.

The limo pulled to the curb. A very large black man stepped out of the back door. His face was contorted in anger.

"No use running, Terry. You got no hiding place from Nicky Baines." The black man's car was blocked by traffic. So Terry took off across Eighth Avenue and ran down Thirteenth Street, running into people, knocking over a little old man with a briefcase.

He ran on, but when he looked back the black man who had spoken to him and another guy, even larger, were gaining on him. Terry saw a garbage truck and ran across the street one second before it turned him into a blot of bloody flesh. It cut them off, gave him a second to think.

Christ, what the hell was he going to do now?

Then he remembered something. What had Valerie Stevenson said at Elaine's? She was doing a photo shoot today, right in this neighborhood. At a studio. High Gloss on Fifth Avenue. Where the hell was that place? Now, he suddenly remembered the giant lizard on the Lone Star café, right across from the studio. He could go there, hang out with her, and make some phone calls. She'd be in his corner. He knew she liked him. Even Thaddeus said so. He could get off the street for a while, tamp down this panic in his brain. Then he could make a more rational decision of what he should do next.

There it was, High Gloss Studios.

He walked through the outer doors but got no farther. An armed security guard with a nose as long and gaunt as a melting icicle stood in his path.

"May I help you, sir?"

"Terry Brennan from *Rolling Stone*. I'm here to write about Valerie Stevenson."

"You have ID, sir?"

Terry pulled out his wallet and showed the guard his license.

"I don't mean that kind of ID sir. I'm talking about a press card."

"*Rolling Stone* writers don't need press cards. Ask anybody in there. They all know me."

At that moment Julie Ho, the photographer's assistant, showed up.

"He's okay, Wayne. Let him in."

The guard reluctantly moved out of Terry's way and Terry walked down into the set. Women's trench coats and black umbrellas were placed strategically all over the room. Plastered on the wall in the background was the Eiffel Tower, with a silhouette of a spy holding a Beretta in her right hand.

"Where's Valerie?" he asked Julie Ho.

"Back there, in the changing room. She's getting ready for the next shot. She's going to look like Modesty Blaise."

"Mind if I go back?"

"Be my guest. Just don't get in the way."

Terry headed back through the make-up artists, the camera assistants. No one paid the slightest attention to him. Which was perfect.

When he saw a door with a sign taped on it. "Changing Room." He rapped gently, but no one answered. They couldn't hear him. Probably due to the radio inside which was blasting Linda Ronstadt doing Buddy Holly's old hit

"That'll Be the Day."

He knocked again but heard nothing. The damned radio. He put his head against the door.

Now he could hear voices coming from the changing room inside.

"That's it, Claudio. Push my head down. Now stick it in…oh God…whip me. It's so big."

Terry felt numbed. He wanted to turn and race out of the place, but it was depressingly fascinating.

"You like it, you little bitch?"

"Yes, Claudio. Oh yes. Um. Whip me with the umbrella."

Terry heard the cracking sound of the umbrella as it hit Valerie's butt. She was screaming now and had taken a break from sucking in order to make a little speech.

"I have never done this before, Claudio. I am a good girl. Too good."

"You never done this with Joey Gardello?"

"Him? You have to be kidding. He thought he was going to marry me. What a joke."

"But I thought you were in love with Joey."

"No, fuck him. He was a violent drug-dealing asshole. You want to know what? He stole three thousand dollars from me. Said he needed it to get his indie movie going. Promised me a part too. I was new in the game and he totally saw me as a mark. I'm glad he's dead."

"Hmm, you *are* a bad girl."

"I am. Very bad. Punish me, Claudio."

Crack, crack…

Squeals of pained delight.

Terry turned and headed out. Through the hallway, past Julie Ho.

"You find her?"

100

"Yeah, but she was busy."

"Shall I tell her you called?"

"Nah," Terry said, as he practically fell out of the door. "Don't bother. Just give my best to Claudio."

He ran out into the street. Jesus, he hadn't realized how much she hated Joey. Why hadn't she told him that night in Elaine's bathroom?

Because she knew he was close to Thaddeus and might tell him? And why wouldn't she want Thaddeus to know?

Maybe she traded on her sweet good looks, but underneath was a seething mass of resentment and out of control ambition like...like Howard.

And—face it—more and more like himself.

The prizes were so big: fame, glory, money.

And failure was so small...the front bar at Elaine's. Looking in and being denied entrance.

Then he thought of Kathy's beautiful face, and more than that. Her strength and character.

What the fuck was wrong with him? How had he ever doubted that she was what he wanted? She was like him. Honest, straight ahead.

Or like he used to be.

Was she still on his side? Would she believe him?

His thoughts were interrupted by a woman in a car who had nearly clipped him as he crossed, daydreaming, on Fifth Avenue.

He staggered on, trying to figure out where to go, and who might help him.

CHAPTER THIRTEEN

Where could he go that that neither Baines' crew nor the cops wouldn't look? Then he saw The Angry Squire, a black radical hangout. The cops wouldn't think he'd duck in there, and certainly none of Nicky's crew. The place was pitch dark. Two black guys in black turtleneck sweaters were at the bar were drinking whiskey. They both had gigantic Afros. They looked at him like they were in a car in the desert and he was a tarantula crossing the road.

He saw the pay phone in the back and reached into his pocket for a dime.

His heart was racing, and he felt bile come up in his throat.

He started to dial Thaddeus, then stopped. It was no use. They'd be all over him. Who could he call? He had so many friends at Elaine's, people hanging all over him, other writers, producers, models, Mick fucking Jagger. Yeah, he could call Mick.

"Hi, Mick, we almost talked last night at Elaine's. Look, someone is setting me up for murder so I wondered if you and Keith could stop by and put in a word for me at my cell on death row. Oh, you're both busy getting blowjobs? Oh, well, maybe tomorrow then? Thanks anyway, man."

Yeah, he knew everybody, but who could he actually

call? Who was really his friend? He was coming up with a big zero.

Then he remembered his agent, Barry Landsman. Yeah, he could call Barry. He was usually straight with him. And he knew everyone in town. He'd have sensible advice, maybe even help him hole up and try to solve what had happened. He dropped in his change.

"Hello, Landsman Agency."

"Hi, Ingrid. It's Terry."

"Terry?" She was practically whispering. "Where in God's name are you? Everyone in Manhattan is trying to find you."

"Yeah, I know. Is Barry there?"

"Just a minute."

He fidgeted in the dark. Saw the bartender looking over at him. Then Terry noticed the television in the corner of the bar. It was on a news channel.

He couldn't have been on the news yet, could he?

Oh Jesus, he thought of how much he wanted to be famous, to have people everywhere know his name and face. It was true. He had come to want the very things he had mocked when he was a professor. He wanted to be a famous celebrity.

And now he would be. The kind of celebrity you saw doing the perp walk to the courthouse, or maybe a celebrity lying in the gutter somewhere, his face full of holes from a "fusillade of police bullets."

"Terry?" came the warm sound of Barry Landsman's deep voice.

"Barry, I'm in a real jam."

"You think so?" Barry said, in his uber-ironic way.

"Don't fuck with me, Barry. I'm serious."

"I hear you, Terry. The cops just left here. They told me if you call that I have to talk you into turning yourself in before things get a lot worse."

"Hey, man, you know I'm clean on this."

"Doesn't matter what I think. The cops seem to think that you were in the coke business with Joey Gardello. They also seem to think you killed him and his brother after you stole their money and drugs. They wanted to know your journalism salary and royalties. I had to tell them, Terry. That you were living from week to week."

"Jesus, thanks, Barry. You realize that you're putting a noose around my neck."

"I can't lie for you, Terry, but I know you didn't ice Joey. The best thing you can do is give up and we'll get you a really great attorney."

"How am I going to do that with no money?"

"I'll front you the money, Terry. I know you're going to get a great bestseller out of this. Now tell me where you are. I'll get the car, come over, and take you in."

Terry felt all the air leak out of his lungs.

Taken into jail. Put behind bars. That would be a great thing for his career. Magazines always like to hire journalists who were former jailbirds.

But what was the alternative?

Stay on the streets and try and find out who did this to him?

Where could he even start? It didn't matter. He had to try.

"Barry, I'll call you back. I have to think about this."

"Terry, come on. Be realistic, man. There's nothing to think about. It's you versus the whole NYPD. They're going to have your picture on the *Times* tomorrow and the *Post* and Sue Simmons at five and even Warner Wolf is going to put you on his sports show because you've done some baseball writing."

"I am not a fucking sportswriter," Terry said, furious.

"Tell me where you are. Don't hang up."

"Shit. The cops are there now, aren't they?" Terry said. "They're trying to trace this call, aren't they?"

"No, no," Barry stuttered. "Just trying to get you to do the right thing. You could end up dead out there. If you guys stole from Nicky Baines…"

"I didn't steal anything," Terry shouted. "I didn't deal any coke. I don't know shit about Joey Gardello's death. Don't you believe me?"

"Of course I do," Barry said. "That was just a slip of the tongue. Though you did tell me that you and Joey were dealing coke out of your place one night. You even called me to see if I wanted to buy some."

Oh Christ, Joey thought. Landsman sounded just like Howard.

"Jesus, did you tell the cops that?"

"Well, they asked me, and I couldn't very well lie, Terry. I mean, we both know you like the wild night life, but all of this can be straightened out. I'm sure of it. The most you will get is a couple of years for dealing, three to five I think. Unless you get busted for Joey's murder. You didn't kill him, did you?"

"Yeah, Barry, I killed him. Right after I whacked Jimmy Hoffa. What the fuck?"

"This is no time for levity, Terry."

"Why not? Seems to be all I got left. You believe me?"

"Oh yeah, sure I do," Landsman said. "No question. They probably won't be able to make the murder charge without a witness. But the drug charge is bad enough. Oh man, Ter, I just thought of something."

"What's that?"

"It might not be three to five after all."

"What? Why not?"

"I forgot about the Rockefeller drug laws. See, judges want to be lenient, but the new laws are so draconian. Yeah, I should have thought of that. You might have to serve ten, T."

"Ten?" Terry felt like he was going to faint. "Ten fucking years?"

"You better come in," Landsman said. "Or they can add resisting arrest and, by the way, what the fuck were you doing punching a policeman?"

Terry felt dizzy, nauseous.

"I gotta go, Barry."

"No, Terry. Listen, I kind of told the cops I'd bring you in. I mean they're counting on me. If they know I talked to you and you didn't listen, they might think I'm involved in this whole mess. They sort of intimated that anyway."

"Oh, I see," Terry said. "Well, it's nice to know you're thinking about my best interests, Barry. You piece of shit."

Terry slammed down the phone, sweat pouring down his face. Who could he call? Who would believe him?

He walked back past the two black men who were drinking what looked like Black Russians. They looked up at him and one of them said, "Cold out there, huh, baby?"

The other one laughed as he staggered outside.

On the garbage-strewn street it had begun to drizzle. He hurried down the block, tried to think. What did a cop tell him one time when he'd done a long piece on a murder in Brooklyn? Start with the victim. Okay. Good idea.

Joey Gardello. Start there. He'd seen Joey more times than he even admitted to himself. To get coke, of course. Joey had come down to his place and sold him the stuff. Then they'd both gotten high, cruised around the Village, gone to the Head.

And there was a guy, a buff black guy, who came to his pad a couple of times with Joey.

Willie Hudson.

Yeah, Willie who worked as a bouncer at Studio 54. Yeah, that was it. They had laughed about it because Willie said he hated disco music. The music he actually dug was doo-wop. They'd gotten really wasted and sung "I Only Have Eyes for You." Willie had a perfect pitch falsetto, and Terry had managed some pretty good bass work.

"I don't know if we're in a garden. Or on a crowded av-a-nue."

A great night.

Cool Willie, as Joey had called him. Maybe he knew something about what happened to Joey. There were no guarantees, but he had to start somewhere.

Oh man, if he could just get to Studio 54 and find him...

Yeah. But there was one problem. If Willie Hudson was the real killer, or if he had double crossed Joey Gardello and set up Terry, then he was one dangerous dude and he had to be stopped.

Terry might hit Howard Freeman in the gut, but Willie was a big guy, a real street dude.

No, to take on Willie he would need a weapon. A fucking gun. Which meant he'd have to break into a gun store somewhere and steal his piece. But what kind? A thirty-eight? A forty-five? He wished he'd listened to his old man, the gun nut, when he was a kid. But he was too busy being a beatnik to learn anything about guns.

He thought guys with guns were straight assholes.

Now he would kill to have a straight asshole friend, instead of a lying, backstabbing ex-hippie shithead like Howard.

He'd have to wait until after nine when all the stores closed. When people were off the street. Then he realized he didn't even know where any gun stores were. He'd need a Yellow Pages. There might be one hanging in the old phone booth on the corner of Barrow and Hudson. But the cops were probably looking out for him there. Or Nicky Baines' boys.

He had to get off the street.

He took a right and crossed Seventh Avenue when he heard the sound of squealing tires. And voices: "There he is. Over there."

"Get his ass."

He looked across the street and watched in horror as a limo pulled up and out of the back came the big black guy and two of his pals. They looked very serious.

Terry saw them coming across the street, so he ran south, leapt over the hood of a parked taxi, and ran for the West Village.

He turned around and saw them racing down Seventh after him.

He ran down the tree lined streets, cut down Bedford, up Hudson, and around the corner to Jane Street. Were they still behind him? He didn't know...

He ducked into the first doorway, stood in the cramped foyer, and waited, waited for them to come.

He watched Hudson Street. They stopped, looked around.

If they came up Jane, he was dead meat.

They looked north, south and up Jane. But after standing there for a few more eternal minutes, they headed west to the docks.

In the doorway, Terry sagged to a sitting position and took deep breaths.

He had to get off the street. Kathy lived only a few houses away. But what if the cops were watching her?

What if she hated him, turned him in?

What difference did it make? It was his last shot.

CHAPTER FOURTEEN

1976—Two Years Earlier

On a cold winter morning, Terry and Thaddeus walked through Central Park until they came to the Sheep's Meadow. There, Terry saw six guys throwing a football around. He recognized a few of them immediately as stars of the hit comedy show "Scream City." Ed Layne, a well-muscled guy with a Harvard sweatshirt on, who was famous for falling down as Gerald Ford. Next to him was Tommy Rizzo, a fat guy who was famous for his physical comedy both on and off the set. Next to them was a fast-rising director, James Randolph, who had just made a fast-paced New York-based cop thriller called *Uptown*. And throwing the ball was a sandy-haired guy named Jerry Wain, a well-known executive at Paramount, who sometimes hung out at Elaine's. Wain was famous for getting pictures made, and Terry immediately saw that this was no ordinary Sunday morning football game. If he played well here maybe it would open some doors. If he didn't...well, he didn't want to think about that at all.

Teams were already established, four on four. Terry was with Thaddeus who quarterbacked their team. In the huddle he looked at Terry.

"You look like a guy who can catch passes."

Terry nodded.

"Okay, here's the play. Go out fast, like you're going to blow right by him. Then stop hard, turn around, like I'm going to throw you a short pass. I'll pump fake to you. That should draw the defensive man in, and you can slip behind him. Then you run like a bat out of hell and I'll float it over his head. On seven."

The team lined up with Terry playing flanker. He was surprised and a little alarmed to find himself guarded by Wain. What the fuck? If he made him look bad that might not be at all good for him. On the other hand, if he faked a fall or a drop he would be an asshole. And everybody would know it anyway.

He looked back at Thaddeus who smiled again. Only this time there was a challenge in his grin. Thaddeus was testing him.

How would he play it?

Thaddeus barked out the signals and the center hiked the ball on seven.

Terry flew out hard, grimacing like he was getting ready for a long run. Then, five yards out, he stopped and turned, opening his hands for a short pass.

Thaddeus, meanwhile, rolled out in his direction, stopped, set his feet and faked the pass. Wain was totally taken in. He came charging up, and jumped in front of Terry, hell bent on intercepting the pass and taking it the other way for six points.

But just as they had laid it out, the short pass never came. Instead, Terry drifted behind him and started running full tilt again. The pass landed in his hands ten yards behind Wain and he jogged the rest of the way to the end zone.

One play. One touchdown.

His team came rushing down to congratulate him. Thaddeus ran downfield and gave him a high five. Wain looked away from him as if nothing had happened. It was clear. He hated him. Well, tough…

"Oh, we are going to have some fun today, Brennan."

Which they did. With Terry and Thaddeus acting as a team, they beat their rivals thirty- five to fourteen. Terry caught three long touchdown passes, and when the game ended, James Randolph asked him if he was interested in playing poker once a month at his place in SoHo. Terry got his phone number. He couldn't have made a better showing.

Even Wain shook his hand in his grudging, superior way.

They walked across to the East Side and ended up at Melons, where they ordered chilled vodka.

Thaddeus clinked glasses with him.

"Unitas to Berry," he said. "Just like the old Colts."

"They were the best."

"You were pretty great today. Did you play in college?"

"Nah. High school but not college. I went to the University of Maryland where they had real jocks on the team. Did you play at Yale?"

"The first year. But I broke my leg in the third scrimmage. It was really a good thing, because it was hard enough coming from the Bronx to the Ivy League."

Terry took out his pad of paper and pen.

"What was so difficult about it?"

"Well the workload was like nothing I'd ever seen in high school. But I could handle that. I think being around rich kids for the first time was the hardest."

"Did they hassle you?"

"No, not physically. No hazing. But they just had much more subtle ways of making you feel like shit. You know, talking about their Christmas vacations in Paris while you were headed back to Co-Op City. Or mentioning their dinners with their parents and the Fords in D.C. They always let you know they were way out ahead of you. That was tough."

"Sounds familiar," Terry said. "I had one student at Hobart who was a so-called hippie. He wanted to live in a commune, so he had his father, who was a big Wall Street guy, buy him one."

Thaddeus cracked up.

"We've got a lot in common," Thaddeus said. "We both went through a lot of the same stuff."

"But I wasn't in Vietnam. I got out because of my heart."

"You have a bad heart?"

"They fixed it later. With an operation. They tell me it's as good as anyone's now."

"Man. Remind me of that the next time you start to do coke."

"I haven't done it much. You're right though. I should never do it. I heard you say you lived the hippie lifestyle for a while."

"Yeah. A year or so. I had a girlfriend though, Leslie. There was no one like her."

A certain look came across Thaddeus' face, a look which Terry knew only too well. The girl who got away.

"What happened to her?"

"She couldn't deal with my, ah, stress syndrome. I was pretty out of it for a while. We just drifted apart. When we broke up is when I came back East. Tried living with my dad in Suffield. Didn't work out too well."

Terry felt an immediate connection with Thaddeus.

"You have a rough relationship with your dad?"

"Not too rough," Thaddeus said. "Let's just say we didn't see eye to eye on much stuff."

"Mine either," Terry said. And felt an ache in his heart.

"No?" Thaddeus said. "That can be rough. And it's a pain that never leaves you. It's funny, whenever I meet someone who tells me about their great relationship with their dad, I feel this instant emptiness. Something you never get over, you know?"

"Yeah, I know."

Terry remembered the time his father had beaten him and threw him down the cellar steps. He had broken two ribs and his right arm. He wanted to tell Thaddeus about it in the most urgent manner, but he managed to shut up. After all, he was the journalist, not the subject.

"Let me ask you something about the book. Did writing it help you face the emotional stuff in your life? I mean did it help you get over 'Nam or the stuff with your dad?"

Thaddeus shook his head.

"No, not really. I'm afraid I don't subscribe to the idea that writing about your emotional scars help you get rid of them. If anything, they can sometimes get worse because there they are on the page, proof that your life is fucked."

"Do you feel that way?"

"No, no…I'm talking theoretically. The truth is I don't let the past hold me back. I use it for my work, yes, but I don't dwell on it all the time when I'm not writing."

"It's great that you can do that," Terry said. "A lot of writers have gotten stuck there."

"I know. That's why I believe in living well now. If you keep moving, you don't have time to get lost in the past."

Terry smiled. That was exactly how he wanted to live. Use the past but don't get shipwrecked by it.

They had another drink and then Thaddeus smiled at him: "You know, Ter," he said. "I don't want you to take this the wrong way, because I'm not saying it to get a positive write up from you. But even in the short time we've known one another I sometimes feel that we're blood brothers."

"Yeah," Terry said. "I know exactly what you mean."

There was a long silence between them. Then Terry blushed a little and quickly called for another round of drinks.

CHAPTER FIFTEEN

1978

Terry walked quickly up the street to Kathy's apartment. Who the hell was he kidding? She probably wouldn't even talk to him.

But he had to give it a try. She was a good person. She was solid. He was sure of it. Well, almost sure of it. She'd help him. Unlike Howard and Landsman, she couldn't leave him out here in the cold.

But then again, what if she had been the one who set him up? That stuff about her apartment being painted. Was that just an excuse to get inside and plant the coke and the money?

Except for one thing. One obvious thing, which, in his haste to find someone to back him, he had almost over-looked. Kathy Anderson—sweet, funny, adorable Kathy—was an actress. He remembered seeing her play a real rat of a woman in a stage version of the old Bette Davis movie *The Letter*. She was terrifyingly convincing as the murder-ess. There was nothing at all left of the sweet, kind Kathy Anderson, All American Girl.

He remembered how stunned he'd been, how total her transformation was.

But who? How could it have worked? Joey steals money and coke from Nicky Baines. Joey needs someone to take the fall, so he gets Kathy to put the coke and money in Terry's apartment.

And Joey did know Kathy. Yes, Joey knew her because, ironically, Terry had introduced them at The Lion's Head, when he'd gone into flirt with her. And she had come over to his place the night Joey was selling coke there. But not for long. She was freaked out by Terry dealing drugs and left in fifteen minutes.

She could be ruled out. Unless that was just an act.

But what choice did he have? He had to go with his gut instinct.

He took a deep breath and decided to trust her. His instincts couldn't be THAT wrong.

Or could they?

He walked up to her address. Rang the buzzer.

"Hello?"

"Kathy. It's me, Terry."

There was a long silence.

"Terry, I don't know any Terry."

"Kathy, wait. I know I screwed up and I'm sorry. But this is serious."

"Oh really? You mean punching a cop when he's trying to arrest you for dealing drugs? That kind of serious?"

"Kathy, I didn't punch anyone. Look, I can explain all of this. Just let me in."

"And become an accomplice?"

He slammed his fist into the door.

"All right. You're right. I have no business coming here. I'll see you around."

He turned to go. But the door buzzed and he quickly

went inside to the hallway before she changed her mind.

She let him in, then stood there in her short Chinese silk robe. She was barefoot, and her hair was pinned up. She looked ridiculously adorable.

"Thanks for letting me in," he said.

"Yeah, right," she said. "Terry, what the hell have you gotten involved in?"

"I don't know," he said, collapsing on her maroon sofa. "Christ, I'm being set up and I don't know why, or who."

His voice trailed off. He was suddenly exhausted.

She stood in front of him, staring down at him with an angry look on her beautiful face.

"Punching cops. Drugs and money found in your place. The cops almost took me in, Terry. As your accomplice! I don't know what to believe."

Terry reached out to her, but she moved away.

"God, I am so sorry. Somebody, somebody knows something. Somebody got the key to…"

He didn't go on. But looked up at her in a suspicious way.

She responded at once.

"Oh you are really good, Terry. You come here, begging me to help you and now you're saying that it was me who set you up?"

"No. I didn't say that. Of course not. Besides you only had the key to my apartment. Whoever set me up had the key to my storage locker downstairs. That's where the drugs and money were found."

She paced back and forth in front of him.

"Of course, there is one thing," Terry said, looking around.

"Tell me, please. I'm dying to hear this."

"Well, I don't see any paint cans, or ladders. You said they were painting your place, but..."

"For Godssake, Terry. The painters got hung up on another job and couldn't make it. But I had no idea of how to get in touch with you, so I went over to your place anyway."

"Uh huh," Terry said. "I see."

"You see? That's great. Wonderful. Okay, I confess. Here's how I did it. I got your apartment key. Then, while I was waiting for nine or ten hours I got really pissed and found your locker key and stuck the drugs and money in there and called the cops on you!"

"No, no...Come on. I'm sorry."

"That's what you were thinking it, weren't you? Oh, and I suppose I only let you in because I'm going to wait for you to fall asleep and then call the cops. I am fucking EVIL!"

She scrunched up her adorable face and wiggled her hands in front of her, the very embodiment of PURE EVIL.

Even though he was exhausted and scared out of his mind, Terry started to laugh.

"I'm sorry," he said. "I am so sorry. I didn't really believe you were involved. Honestly, I'm not thinking straight. That's all."

"I'll say," she said, her hands on her hips. "Let me remind you, Terry, that you have been chasing me, not the other way around. I won't ask why you didn't call me at your place. Because I already know. You thought I was on one phone while my new buddies the cops were listening in. I was going to set you up so they could take you in!"

God, she was bright. This was, of course, exactly what he'd been thinking.

"No, no, of course not, Kath. I just got confused. I went to Joey's funeral and…"

"You went to that slimebag's funeral? How interesting!"

"No, not for myself. But for Thaddeus. He asked me to. You know that Joey was his best friend."

"His best friend? Joey Gardello, the spineless drug dealer?"

"You seem to like him just fine when I introduced you to him at the Head."

Now Kathy began to walk back and forth in front of him like a District Attorney in front of a hostile witness.

"Oh yeah, Terry, I adored Joey I wanted to crawl into his lap. Hmm, wonderful, erotic Joey."

She assumed a super erotic pose and shut her eyes as though she was dreaming of an all-night sexual liaison with Joey. Terry winced at the thought.

But Kathy leaped from that pose to an accusatory stance. Legs spread, hands on hips.

"You jerk! I was polite and smiled at him because that was my freaking job. Do you understand? I smile at any customer who buys a drink, even you!"

Terry double winced.

"And another thing," Kathy said, staring down at him with dragon wrath. "How do I know you aren't a big-time drug dealer who actually did all the stuff the cops are accusing you of? You admit you let Joey sell people drugs out of your apartment a couple of times. Did you make a profit on those deals? Maybe you really did kill him and took his drugs and now you're thinking about somehow involving me. I could be *your* patsy."

"Look," he said. "I've been pretty mixed up but I'm not anymore. I'm crazy about you. Okay?"

Shit, he hadn't meant to say that. Though it was true.

"Oh, bullshit," she said. "Giant tons of bullshit. You stood me up and now you're desperate and you think that saying you love me will get you over? You are so demented. And yet so obvious. Really. I don't believe a word of it. Not one word."

"You do too," Terry said. "I've been an idiot, but you know I would never deal coke. And you know I would never kill anyone, even a shit like Joey."

"Why should I believe you?" she said. "And you *did* deal coke. From your own little apartment. Liar!"

"No, I didn't deal it. I just let a few friends come over and score a little. Joey made all the money. I was doing him a favor is all. I just supplied an, ah…affable environment."

"A what? That's so pathetic. Tell that to the cops when they take you away! And why did you even let him use your pad if you hated him so much?"

"I did it because he was Thaddeus' best friend and I thought I should like him. Thaddeus wanted us all to get along. Be pals."

"Like a band of brothers, I suppose?"

"I know it sounds lame but that's what I wanted. You know, artistic friends. Like Hemingway and Fitzgerald."

"More like Bugsy Siegel and Meyer Lansky!"

Terry started to laugh again. She had such a great wit. So what if her legs weren't as long as Valerie's? You couldn't trade banter with legs.

"Now, you are in a real mess, Mr. Brennan," she said. "And you want me to risk everything to hide you out here. Meanwhile, you are going to do what?"

"First, I've got to find this Willie Hudson, Joey's old friend. He works at Studio 54 as a bouncer."

"And you think he might be the one who set you up?"

"I don't know. Maybe. But even if he's not, he might know who did."

"And exactly who is this Willie thug?"

"I only met him a couple of times. He was Joey's friend from the movie world, an ex-actor who wanted to become a director. But he hasn't gotten anywhere yet."

Kathy threw her hands into the air in a remarkable display of theatrical contempt.

"Oh, good. Wonderful. Another loser like Joey. And you're going to do what, the same thing you did just now with me? Walk into Studio 54 and say, 'Hi, Willie, say, buddy, did you set me up for drug-dealing and murder and, if so, would you please come along with me to the local police station and confess? Thanks a lot, pal.'"

"Not exactly like that," Terry said, realizing he hadn't thought all this out very well. In his magazine gigs he felt his way along and made instant adjustments to get people to talk. He'd sort of assumed it would be the same deal with Willie, but, of course, Willie might have weapons, probably would have them, many of them. Maybe he wouldn't like the direct technique or, in fact, any of Terry's techniques.

"Let me ask you a question, Terry? Do you have a gun?"

"A gun?" Terry said. "Ah, no, but I had planned on getting one before I saw Willie. Goes without saying."

"And where would you obtain this weapon, may I ask?"

"I have my contacts. In the Bronx," Terry added, suddenly remembering a couple of guys he had interviewed up there for a crime story two years ago.

"Oh, I see. You were going to go up there first and get the gun and then go see Willie, the massively muscled bouncer, and do what? Stick the gun in his ear?"

"No, not exactly that," Terry said. "I had other plans. But I can't divulge them just now."

Kathy walked up and down in front of him like a district attorney.

"Yeah, I bet. Have you ever done anything that required physical bravery in your entire life?"

"Hell, yes. I played lacrosse in college."

"A plus for you, but that doesn't cut it against Nicky Baines! Let me ask you another question. Do you even have any idea how to shoot a gun?"

"I object. Ridiculous question," Terry said. "Absurd. Do I know how to shoot a gun? Really, I can't believe you asked me that."

Kathy smiled, leaned down and stared into his eyes.

"Do you even know where the safety is on a pistol?"

Terry hoped his face wasn't turning rubber-ball red.

"Absurd question and I feel no need whatsoever to comment. None."

"Evasive answer," Kathy said, striding up and down in front of him again.

"You obviously have never shot a weapon. You have no knowledge of even the most rudimentary aspects of the handgun. You will, when you come up against Willie Hudson, or Nicky Baines, be a sitting duck, a stuffed goose and one dead motherfucker."

"That is completely and totally wrong," Terry said. "In so many ways. First of all, I do know quite a bit about handguns."

"Really?"

"Yeah, really."

"Okay, tell me something interesting about the Colt ACP."

"Ah," Terry said. "The ACP. One of my very favorite weapons."

"Really? Tell me what ACP stands for."

"Come on," Terry said. "That's so easy. Kath. I mean, ACP, come on. That's a kindergarten gun question."

"Fine, Mister Badass. Tell me."

"As any aficionado knows, ACP stands for Air-Cooled Pistol."

Kathy responded with a simultaneous laugh-slash-smirk.

"Air-cooled pistol? You sure it isn't Air-Conditioned Pistol?"

"It could be," Terry said. "All right, Honey West. What is it?"

"Automatic Colt Pistol. At least you got 'pistol' right. 'Air-cooled pistol.' That's a good one. Man, you really do need help."

She went to the closet and pulled out a hat box. She opened it and took out a handgun wrapped in blue velvet.

"Here it is, Terry. The very same Colt."

"Wow," Terry said, holding the gun. "You are some kind of woman."

"Yes, I am," Kathy said. "And I can shoot the spots off of a leopard too."

"You serious?"

Kathy looked at him and winked.

"You bet. My father took me out to the range when I was eight. We competed as a team with the adults by the time I was twelve. I've won many medals."

"That's great. How about loaning it to me?"

"What for? You'd only shoot some innocent bystander."

"No, I wouldn't. When I find Willie, I'd just hold it on him. He won't know I can't hit the side of a barn."

"Yes, he will," she laughed.

"How?"

"'Cause your hand will be trembling. It's a scary thing to hold a gun on someone."

Terry held out his hand.

"Let me show you just how steady I am."

Before Kathy could hand it to him, they heard footsteps in the hallway.

Kathy put her forefinger over her lips.

They crept toward the door together, the gun still in Kathy's hand.

They heard a voice, whispering: "You think they're in there?"

"Only one way to find out."

"We don't have a warrant."

"Tough."

Kathy looked at Terry and nodded her head to the side of the apartment.

They climbed down the fire escape as fast as they could. Kathy had her handbag with the Colt inside. Once out on the street they heard a siren approaching her front entrance.

"You should go back," Terry said. "They don't have anything on you."

"Did you hear the way those guys were talking?" she said. "I'm not giving myself up to those two guys. I'm not even sure they'd bother to take me in to the station. There's something not right here, Terry."

"Which is just what I was telling you. This whole thing stinks and this guy Willie, he's the only one who knows anything. I gotta get to Studio 54 and talk to him now."

"I'm going with you," Kathy said.

"What? No way."

"Sorry. I have to protect my gun."

"Oh, your gun? That's nice to hear but…"

"Shut up, Terry. We have to get to the subway."

She clicked together the clasp on her handbag and started off fast across the street. Terry tripped on the curb and almost fell down. She turned and shook her head:

"Come on Marlowe," she said. "Before they fry us both."

CHAPTER SIXTEEN

1976—Two Years Earlier

Jake's was the hottest bar in downtown Manhattan. Movie stars, writers, Warholians, punk rockers, and painters crowded into the place at night. The bathroom had so many people using it for cocaine sniffing that sometimes a line curled out the door.

Terry showed up at lunchtime and found Gina Wade, Thaddeus' assistant, already sitting at a banquette drinking a flute of champagne. She was dressed, as always, like a 1940s literary luminary in a green tweed-wool suit. Her hair was cut short and she had on her round-lensed glasses.

He liked her look but there was something a little too made up about her. It was almost as if she were in costume. Playing a role from another era.

"I was surprised you wanted to meet here," Terry said, "I didn't know this was one of your hangouts."

"I love it here. Patrick, the owner, is an old friend. I used to write my column for the *Voice* from here a few years back."

"Which you gave up."

"New editor didn't like my work. Said I was too literary."

"But you're in the NYRB now," Terry said. "Much

127

classier."

"Yes, but it hardly keeps me in pasta. I like your work in *Rolling Stone*."

"Thanks," Terry said. Looking at Gina now, he found her very attractive. Her eyes shone with intelligence and wit. And yet there was something cool and a little scary about her eyes. Like she was sizing you up to see if you were worth her time. He ordered a glass of champagne for himself and then took out his notepad.

"You met Thaddeus at Yale?"

"Yes, I was working on a novel, a novel about a painter. Well, I shouldn't say a novel. That sounds as though I've written it. The truth is I'm still working on it. I write fifty pages, then I go back and throw it out as the rubbish it is."

"I doubt that," Terry said. "So where did you actually meet him?"

Gina smiled and shook her head.

"We met in New York, standing in front of a painting. We started talking and the odd thing was we were both students at Yale. We'd both come to the city and met by coincidence. Thaddeus had such interesting things to say about it that we had lunch together. And we've been together ever since."

Something clicked in Terry's mind.

"Was the artist Jackson Pollack, by chance?"

"How did you know that?" She took out a pack of Lucky Strikes, the same brand which Thaddeus smoked.

"It's weird. I met Thaddeus at the Modern a few days back and he was looking at a Jackson Pollack painting. We had a good conversation about it."

Gina laughed.

"The dear guy," she said. "He went that day on my

account. I was stuck trying to describe those numbered paintings and I asked him if he got a chance to look at them and give me his impressions, which I would then steal and put into my novel."

They both laughed, but Terry felt a touch of the illicit pass between them.

"That's pretty unusual," Terry said. "A world class novelist acting as a researcher. I don't think I've heard of anything like that before."

"Well, remember, he wasn't a world class anything when we met. Anyway, you ought to ask him about his opinions about how art is created. Thaddeus believes that no art is a single person's creation. Every great artist had his circle, his friends who helped educate him. More than any formal school. Think of the romantics, or Picasso and his circle, or Hemingway and Fitzgerald. None of them would have created what they did without that input, that spiritual sustenance they gained from their comrades."

"But what of the myth of the unsullied single genius?"

"I'm glad you said 'myth,'" Gina said. "Because that's all it is."

Terry felt a great sympathy sweeping through him. This really was amazing. He thought about keeping it to himself, but it was the kind of thing he simply had to share.

"It's so funny," he said. "I've always believed the exact same thing. One of the reasons I left academia was that there was no circle of writers to be with. Just me among the academics. I've always dreamed of hanging out with other writers, learning from them. I'm not talking about Brook Farm, nothing that idyllic, but just a give and take, in a creative, serious way. I guess that sounds corny and absurd."

Gina smiled in a knowing way and blew smoke out of both nostrils.

"Totally corny," she said. "And stunningly absurd. But also refreshingly honest and lovely. And, from what I've seen, it's true, too. But do keep it a secret. If any of the ultra-ironists in the New York writing scene hear about out secret coven of brotherly and sisterly love they'd banish us to Jersey."

"I promise," Terry said. "I must say it's so great to hear you feel as I do. I sometimes think I'm an idiot for believing this stuff."

"Well, since you've told me your deep secret, I'll tell you one. Thaddeus thinks you're great too. He was speaking about how much fun it is hanging out with you doing the story. And believe me he doesn't often say such things about journalists. He despises most of them."

"That's kind of him to say," Terry said. But his antennae rose a little. Was she just telling him all this, so he'd write an upbeat profile of Thaddeus?

Of course, it was possible. But thinking back on what had just transpired between them he doubted her insincerity. After all, it had been she who had brought up the circle of friends as being instrumental to an artist's development. Not himself.

"Thaddeus is such a confident person," Terry said. "Has he always been that way?"

Gina looked at him in a querulous manner.

"Not at all," she said, after a long hesitation. "When we were in Creative Writing classes at Yale, he was just the opposite. In fact I had to practically threaten him to hand in his first short story."

"Really?"

"Yes, really. He was certain he would be laughed out of the school. But I stayed up with him all night, trying to buoy his nerve. Finally, I told him if he didn't hand it in, I'd steal it and give it to our professor myself."

"Do you remember what it was about?"

"Funny, now that you mention it, I do. It concerned four friends who grew up together. Well, one of them anyway. The others were only mentioned. It was fairly melodramatic. Our hero is an existentialist who considers suicide. Influenced, by Hemingway and Camus."

"It sounds like a rough version of his novel."

"Yes, doesn't it? Took years to get from that story to the book the whole world loves."

"But he did it," Terry said.

"He certainly did," Gina said. "And given his family life, against all odds."

"His father?"

"How did you know? Thaddeus usually doesn't talk about that."

"He told me a little, but I had the feeling that what he went through was much worse than he told me."

"It was. His father was a talented painter, but he never got anywhere because he attacked people who wanted to help him. The booze and pills he took made him paranoid. He used to beat Thaddeus regularly. It was very bad."

"I guessed it," Terry said.

"I wonder how?" Gina said.

But she looked as though she already knew.

"You two are brothers, Terry. Star crossed."

Terry smiled. These were his people. He had found the artistic home he'd always dreamed of.

"Well, I've got to get along," she said. "I'm having some

friends over tonight. Just a few dull super literary types. Poets, if you must know the truth. Thaddeus won't be seen with them. And I'm sure you'd find it dreary as well. But I like the way some of them think. Cakes and ale…"

She smiled and got up from her chair.

Then she surprised Terry by hugging him tight.

"If you need anything else for your piece, just call."

"I will. Thanks so much."

"Oh, it was fun," she said. "Like everyone else I enjoy seeing my name in print. Especially from such a distinguished journalist."

She kissed him on the cheek and squeezed his arm, then made her way toward the door.

CHAPTER SEVENTEEN

1978

Kathy and Terry stood across the street from the mob waiting to be admitted to Studio 54. There were people wearing Big Bird costumes and an old lady dressed in a mini-skirt and roller skates. She must have been eighty. Then there were two girls dressed in nothing but strategically placed glitter. There were two identical twins dressed in orange plastic hard hats like the Village People. And interspersed with them were forty or fifty preppie types, the kind of kids who came down from Yale. They usually got in because, however wild the scene was, Steve Rubell and Ian Schindler, the club's owners, wanted classy New Yorkers to be part of the freak show mix. Dotted among the crowd were the Bridge and Tunnel people, just like at Elaine's. The only difference was at Elaine's they were at least able to get in, stand at the bar and pretend they were a part of the hip crowd but here at the Studio they couldn't get in at all. Terry heard one woman whining to Rudy the gatekeeper, "Look how I'm dressed. You need a Raggedy Ann in there, doncha?" It was true. She had on overalls and a red and black striped shirt and her hair was dyed red and she wore clown shoes, green sneakers several sizes too big. She was a perfect fool of a Raggedy Ann, but that cut no soap with Rudy, who shook his head and yelled, "No, no, no, that outfit doesn't make it at all. This isn't fairyland, lady. Back of the line." The woman's over-made-up face sagged and she looked as though she was going to turn into a puddle of tears. The crowd pushed her aside as more people came pouring in from behind her.

"Well, Nick Charles, this was your idea. Now how the hell the hell are we going to get through this mob of mental patients?" Kathy said.

"I don't know," Terry said. "It's all up to our boy there."

"Haven't you been here before?" Kathy said. "I thought you were Mister Night Clubber."

"I did get in once," Terry said. "But that night I was with a famous celebrity."

"Really, who?"

"Guy I met at Elaine's. We really hit it off. He gets in anywhere."

"Who is it?"

"Mikhail Baryshnikov. Misha."

"You're kidding me. You hang out with him?"

"Once in a while. I wish he was here now."

"Who is that over there? Those two people. They're kind of looking at you."

Terry looked across 54th Street and saw four people getting out of a stretch limo. It was a couple he knew, not well, but he had shared a bottle of champagne with them a few weeks ago. African wildlife guru Peter Beard and one of his many supermodel girlfriends. And now, getting out behind them, were Mick Jagger and Bianca. She of the flashing teeth and Ultimate Cheekbones.

"Come on," Terry said, tugging at Kathy's arm. "Now

or never."

Terry pushed his way through the crowd, knocking down a man dressed like a cowboy, but with assless pants.

"Peter," Terry cried. "Hey, man. Good to see you."

Beard, always affable in an unflappable way, turned and looked at Terry with a confused grin.

"Brennan," he said. "You going in?"

"Yeah. I hope."

"Come with us. You know Mick and Bianca, right?"

Terry smiled and nodded. Mick looked at him and nodded in a friendly way. Bianca flashed her killer smile and Terry felt a surge of jealousy and celeb worship that made him sick to his stomach. You could tell yourself that these people meant nothing, but in their presence you realized just how unimportant you yourself were.

But there was no time for self-hatred at the moment. He just had to hang onto Kathy and push his way through the screaming, tumultuous crowd, as the Red Sea parted and he and Kathy were let in for free, with the Gods and Goddesses of the night.

Once inside they were quickly separated from their benefactors by a swarming group of people who were forming a half-naked conga line around the ballroom. Kathy was nearly run over, but Terry grabbed her in the nick of time, holding her close to him as the dancers lurched by. By the time they had recovered they saw that Beard and crew were already sitting down on the celeb couches on the far wall. Sitting with them were Andy Warhol, and...could it be...yes, Betty Ford.

"If you're famous enough you can sit with anyone, I guess," Kathy said.

The disco music, The Bee Gee's doing "Stayin Alive,"

was so amazingly loud that Terry could feel his heart synching up with the bass. Indeed it was like his heart WAS the bass or had been replaced by it. His skin seemed to pulsate in and out in and out as the screaming music completely overwhelmed him.

"Gotta find Willie," Terry screamed into Kathy's ear.

She nodded and they made their way through the pulsating, strobe-lit dancers, a kind of hell-on-earth madness on everyone's face.

Was this fun? It didn't seem so to Terry. He hated the music more than anything he'd ever heard. He looked and saw three people snorting coke in the corner, their little vials in their hands. They were laughing wildly, and started dancing like mad robots, their hands flailing around like they were batting away giant mosquitoes.

They came to a flight of steps which led to the upstairs. There were half-naked bus boys running drinks up and down the stairs and when he took a few steps he had to step over a gay couple who were having sex against the leather railings. One man was bent over the rail while the other one screwed him from behind. Kathy and Terry politely worked their way around them. "Beg your pardon, sir," Kathy said. She moved around their jack-hammering bodies in a dainty manner, smiling at them like someone's maiden aunt.

They reached the top balcony and watched as two couples screwed in tandem up against the rail. People were snorting, dancing, screwing, and sucking one another freely, without the slightest self-consciousness.

Terry tried to move through them, kept looking around.

Finally he and Kathy found an open spot where they could lean against the rail themselves and look down at the dance floor.

"Jesus, what a madhouse." Terry said.

"Fuck Willie. Let's get undressed and screw," Kathy said.

"Oh man, do we have to?"

She laughed at him.

"What's this guy look like?"

"What the fuck you two doing here?"

Terry turned and looked at the purple strobe-lit face of Willie Hudson.

"Looks like him," he said.

In Willie's hand was a small automatic.

"You two come with me now. Down the steps. And don't try nothing individualistic, okay? 'Cause I will shoot your asses dead."

They made their way through the writhing bodies and eighty-year-old Rollerina, who was now being passed from dancer to dancer, as Donna Sumner cooed "love to love you, baby." Then they were going down more leather-padded railings into a dark lower depth, where Willie let them into a small room with couches, a couple of chairs, and a mini-bar.

"This here is the Very Very Important Persons Room," he said. "I figure you looking for me."

"How'd you know that?" Terry said.

"The cops looking for you. I see it on the tube. Sister Sue Simmons said you dealing coke with Joey and maybe you offed his ass."

"That's not it, man," Terry said. "You know I didn't do any of that. Somebody is setting me up."

"I don't know shit. You could be the one who did Joe

and Ray and then you come here to make the cops think I done it."

"Did you?" It was Kathy speaking.

"How you involved in this?" Willie said, moving the gun on her.

"I'm Terry's bodyguard," Kathy said, nodding toward Terry.

"Okay, I think about this and I kind of trust you too. You a writer. You his girlfriend from the Lion's Head, right?"

"How did you know that?"

"'Cause I went in there a couple of times with Joey. We all got high at Terry's place one night. I recognize you. You an actress, right?"

"That's right," Kathy said. "Once in a while."

"Okay, I hear that. Look, I know you two dints do shit," Willie said. "I heard Joey talking about you. He was jealous of your relationship to his old buddy. You come here thinking maybe I offed him, stole his dope, then tried to set you up?"

"We weren't sure what to think," Terry said. "I was hoping maybe you could help me."

"Yeah, right. Dig, I don't know who did it, but I gotta guess it was Nicky. Joey mighta possibly been involved in ripping off one of his coke trucks."

"Jesus," Terry said. "I knew Joey was fucking headed for trouble, but ripping off Nicky? That's beyond dumb, man."

"I know, way beyond. But he had something else planned, too."

"Yeah?"

"Yeah, the coke thing, he asked me if I would ever go

into a robbery with him. I said no. But he say he got to get some bread to hang in there for about six more months. Then he going to be on easy street."

"He had something big set up? What, a movie?"

"Naw. Wasn't that. If he had a movie set up, he woulda told me for sure. It wasn't no movie deal, but he wouldn't say what it was. Look, I wish I could tell you, 'cause the cops rousted me already."

"Shit. There must be somebody who knows what the fuck Joey was up to."

"There is. I mean there was."

"Who?"

Kathy looked at Terry: "He means Ray."

Willie nodded solemnly.

"Only person Joe ever really trusted was his bro. He would tell him all kinds of shit. My guess is whoever offed him knew that. Which is why they took 'em both out at once."

They all sat stock still seemingly at a dead end. Then Willie spoke up.

"Hey, there is somebody else."

"Who?" Kathy said.

"Rosalie Torres. His ex."

"I know Rose," Terry said. "But they were divorced."

"Yeah, but he still confided in her, you know? He used to call her late at night to tell her his troubles and shit. She was like his moms or something."

"Hey, it's worth a shot," Terry said.

"I got her number here," Willie said, taking a small phone book out of his hip pocket. "Nice lady. Joey fucked that up good."

"Sounds like Joey fucked everything up," Kathy said.

"That's correct," Willie said. "He did. Fucking things up was J's specialty."

They heard something then. A sound. Footsteps, coming their way...

Then a harsh, loud voice: "Open the fuck up in there."

"The cops?" Terry whispered.

"Oh shit," Willie said. "Worse. Those are brothers. My guess is that they're here for me from Nicky. They just two doors away. We gotta make it out the back way. Come with me."

They got up and followed him out of the Very Important Persons Room to the dark back hall.

"This way," Willie said. He ran them down the hall away from the sound of men kicking in doors and screaming, "Put your hands behind your head!"

At the end of the hall they found another door, which said No Admittance. Willie opened it and shoved them inside. There were massive furnaces and pipes, the internal combustion engine of Studio 54.

"Through here," Willie said.

They ran through the airless cellar, the sound of the booming disco bass slamming through the giant boilers and cooling units.

Then, behind them, they heard the sound of men yelling to one another.

"In here. Mutherfuckers just came through here."

"Shit," Willie said. "They be on to us. But we okay. Keep this if we get separated."

He wrote out Rosalie's address on a scrap of paper and handed it to Terry.

They made a turn and there was a door marked Exit.

"Up these steps and we come out on 54th Street,"

Willie said.

He turned the lock and opened the door.

There were a set of steps which led up to an outside door.

"Come on." Willie said.

He opened the door and two big black men waited for him. One of them hit him in the stomach hard and Willie doubled over with pain. But when the guy attempted to hit him again, Willie kicked him hard in the knee. The man howled and fell backwards.

Willie grabbed the second man and held on.

"Go," he said.

"But you…"

"Get your asses outta here."

He kicked the second guy in the shins. The man howled.

Terry grabbed Kathy's hand and they cut around the battle and headed uptown for the subway.

CHAPTER EIGHTEEN

Clarence Eberhard finished his day delivering mail in tiny Caldwell, New Jersey. The neighborhood he delivered in, Park Avenue and the surrounding streets, featured fine old homes, some built as far back as 1900. Great looking old places with big, wide front porches with comfy chairs on them. Places owned by doctors and businessmen, and well, he didn't know them all personally, but one thing they all had in common was they were rich.

Unlike himself.

No, after he made his way back to the post office, he went to the little parking lot and got into his battered old Nash Ambassador.

How he hated this car. Which cornered like a tank.

But with his lousy pay at the post office and his ever-increasing rent at his crummy little apartment complex, Dutch Village, he really couldn't afford to buy another car.

This was his lousy life: his lousy job delivering mail, working for his psycho boss, The Mad Hun, Timothy Schmidt, and living in Dutch Village, which featured a broken, falling-down picture of a Dutch woman wearing traditional peasant costume in front of the entrance, a clapboard windmill with chipped cream paint. The whole joint depressed him big time.

But not as mightily as the broken toilet in his horrible little apartment or the rats he found nibbling at the electric wires which caused all manner of blackouts.

Even so, Clarence could have borne all of these humiliations if his girlfriend Anne hadn't left him for his former best friend, Pinky Wilson, a milkman.

A milkman!

Surely on the great scale of things a milkman was lower than a mailman.

But they had all gone out bowling one night and Pinky had bowled strike after strike and so Annie fell for him, just like that.

Which meant he couldn't go to Starlite Lanes anymore either. He'd tried it one time and faked a big "Hiya, guys!" but the pain from pretending was like some kind of steak knife in his back and neck.

Yes, his life sucked big time.

Indeed, the only thing he looked forward to was his collection.

His collection of celebrity magazines made him almost happy. He could go into his crowded little bedroom and then slide out his carefully stored cardboard boxes of magazines from under his bed. Then he could sink down into his comfy old chair, and slowly, with growing excitement, he'd take the tops off the boxes and delve into the wonderful goodies inside. All his celeb magazines. From now all the way back to the 1950s, and even some from the '40s. There they were, pages to dream on, pictures of the great stars, stories about their lives. *People Magazines*, *Interview*, *GQ*, *Modern Screen*, *Photoplay*, *Show Biz*, *16 Magazine*, and *Tiger Beat*.

Drinking a Rolling Rock and sitting down in his zebra

striped PJs. Clarence could spend hours and hours losing himself in trivia about stars of his youth…Bobby Sherman, Davey Jones, and so many others. Or the true greats like Liz Taylor, and Richard Burton and Michael Caine.

And now he had some new favorites, favorites he had discovered on his own by going into Elaine's twice a month.

People like authors. He hadn't read many books but when he was at the bar one night and the restaurant wasn't crowded, he could actually hear Norman Mailer, the author of some big best-selling books, talking to that handsome young guy, also a writer, Thaddeus Bryant.

Geez, the way those guys could talk about anything. History or movies, or books, or women, jumping from one thing to another. They were super-brilliant.

And that was one thing that was so cool about Elaine's.

Sure, you went there to see actors and rock stars like Julie Christie and Rod Stewart or Mick. But if you listened closely you actually learned stuff.

You learned that writers like Mailer hung out with boxers like Jose Torres and even knew Muhammad Ali, who came in once in a while. You learned that Thaddeus Ryan's best friend used to be this guy Joey but was now the journalist Terry Brennan. That Brennan had written a piece in *Rolling Stone* saying how cool Bryant was and now Bryant was trying to help him get famous by letting him hang around Elaine's with him.

So that's how fame worked. If you did something for a famous person maybe they would make you famous too.

This guy Thaddeus was so cool. He had that amazing supermodel with him, Shelby Jones. God was she gorgeous.

It made him go out and buy Thaddeus' book, *The Debt*. So far he had read thirty-seven pages in three weeks.

It was really great too. Though he had to stop and look up big words in it.

But he did it. He looked them all up and wrote them down.

Clarence had dropped out of community college five years ago, but he was getting an education from his hobby.

Though he didn't like the word "hobby."

He felt that going into New York and hanging out at the bar was much more.

He was part of...okay, not quite part of...but *almost* part of a world of superstars, the most talented and wonderful people in the world.

He was there at the bar and someday, one day one of them would notice him.

It would happen. He was sure of it.

Okay, he wasn't sure sure, but he had this feeling about Thaddeus Bryant. Bryant had smiled at him and given him a thumbs up recently as they passed each other in front of the place.

He knew Clarence existed. Now, he had to be ready for the day he helped Thaddeus.

He had no idea exactly how this would come about but, hey, if he could help that suck-up journalist Brennan then why not Clarence?

It would happen.

Say, like, Thaddeus choked on a piece of food. And no one else there knew the Heimlich maneuver. Aha...but he, Clarence Eberhard, did know it.

Oh yes he did.

He knew it and knew it well. 'Cause you had to learn it at the post office.

And so there's Thaddeus lying there gagging on the floor,

and does Terry Brennan know what to do? Absolutely not.

And Elaine is in a panic, waving her arms around, and big shots like Richard Harris and Julie Christie are there, and do they know?

Uh-huh. No way, Jose.

And out comes Clarence, emerging from the bar mob and he says the following: "Stand back, please. Help me get him on this chair."

And they drag Thaddeus onto the chair and Clarence places his hands around him from behind, then clasps his big hands together and give a good squeeze, using the upward motion. Does it once, twice, and then boom, third time's the charm.

Thaddeus shoots out a big bone from a pork chop and seconds later, he's breathing and swallowing just fine.

And Clarence is a hero.

A freaking hero and he's being interviewed by the same magazines he's got here in his bedroom. *GQ* and *Esquire* and he's on *Entertainment Tonight*!

He'll be a player. A winner.

They won't laugh at him in freaking Caldwell anymore.

He'd be able to get into the main dining room at Elaine's.

"Hey, Clarence," Mick would say.

"What's shaking, C," Woody Allen would say.

Julie Christie would kiss him as he came in, lay her million-watt smile on him.

God, with his eyes closed, he could almost feel it happening now. He wasn't in this trashed-out dump anymore but sitting in the back with the real people, the people who counted.

And not only with them.

He was one of them, a hero, a person other envied and

emulated and wanted to know.

Man, with his eyes squeezed shut so tight, he really was only a step away.

CHAPTER NINETEEN

The subway roared up the West Side toward the Bronx. Terry and Kathy found themselves practically alone in the car. They sat together, Terry's arm around her, both of them tense.

"I hope Rosalie can help us," Terry said. "Jesus, those guys grabbing Willie. I don't like to think what they're going to do to him."

"Me either," Kathy said.

There was an abandoned *New York Post* sitting on the bench next to her. She picked it up in a reflexive way and sat it on her lap.

"You think about this?" she said to Terry.

"What?"

"Let's say we get up to Rosalie's and she does actually know what happened to both the money and the coke."

"Okay," Terry said.

"Well, what do we do then, smart guy? Put the coke in a cake box and the money in a shopping bag and head over to Nicky's glamorous place, wherever the hell that is, and knock on the door? 'Hi there, we're just a couple of whacky kids who would like to give you back the coke and the money which, by the way, we didn't steal.' What the shot of him believing us? More important what's the shot of either of us walking out of there with our arms and legs attached to our bodies?"

"You don't think he'd believe us?"

"No, I don't. And neither do you."

"Hey, he might not believe me, but you have such a winning smile."

Kathy made a sour face and shook her head.

"Well, I guess we could take it to the police," Terry said.

"Right," Kathy said. "And they wouldn't arrest us. No way. They'd probably give us a Good Citizen's Medal."

Terry sighed. Of course she was right. Either way, they were screwed. But it seemed the only line of action worth taking.

He reached over and tried to take Kathy's hand, but she had started reading the paper, so he tried thinking of what he'd say to Rosalie Torres when they found her. He had barely scratched the surface of his plan when he was smacked hard in the face.

"What the fuck?' Terry yelled, rubbing his stinging cheek. "Something wrong with you?"

"Yeah," Kathy said. "*This* is what's wrong with me."

She pointed to the front page of the *New York Post*.

"Journalist Hunted by Cops for Coke and Murder Scam."

He looked under the headline and saw a blown-up picture of himself coming out of the Men's Room at Elaine's with Valerie Stevenson a few nights back. He had a smudge of white powder under his nose and a ridiculously guilty look on his face. Valerie's dress was messed as was her hair, which hung over her left eye in an impossibly sexy Veronica Lake look.

Kathy pulled the paper out of his hands and began to read loudly: "Freelance Journalist Terry Brennan is being hunted by the NYPD as a person of interest in a combined cocaine theft and the murder of his former partner Joseph Gardello of 118 West 76th Street and his brother Raymond Gardello of Arthur Avenue in the Bronx. The two brothers are suspected of dealing cocaine stolen from Harlem dealer Nicky Baines. According to unnamed sources, Brennan, then stole the cocaine from the Gardello brothers then killed both of them in a double homicide in Central Park, one week ago."

"Total bullshit," Terry said, as the train pulled into their stop.

"Of course it is," Kathy said. "And you and that that whore model coming out of the men's room together, I suppose that's all bullshit too. Tell me how it's a composite picture, Terry."

"Look, I can explain that."

"Of course you can," Kathy said. "You are great at explaining things. Though I don't call it 'explaining.' I call it lying, you bastard."

"Listen, Kath…wait," Terry stuttered.

But it was no use. Kathy was out of the stopped subway car and was running up toward the crossover which was headed back downtown.

"Wait, where are you going?" Terry said, as he ran after her.

"I don't know. I can't go to my apartment. I'll think of something. Meanwhile, I am going to forget that any of this happened. Why I believed you about anything I'll never know. And I was ready to risk my life to help you. And what would I get if by a miracle we did get out of this?

Kicked to the curb by Mister Cool so he could run off with his goddamned moronic model."

Kathy was crying now, and Terry wanted to do nothing more than hold her in his arms and explain to her that he was mad about her and would never leave her. But when he tried to hold her, she wriggled away, screaming.

"Get away from me. You try and touch me one more time and I'll call the cops. I mean it!"

She turned away. Terry started after her again.

"But, Kathy, the cops know who you are. You need to be with me."

"No way. I'll go to my sister's in New Jersey."

Tears rolled down her face and over her luscious lips.

Terry couldn't stand it any longer. He moved toward her with open arms.

But Kathy slapped his hand down, turned and ran away.

CHAPTER TWENTY

Terry thought about running after her. His heart was aching, and he feared that he had really done it this time. Lost her forever.

But there was no going back now. The only way he could prove to her and to everyone else that he was innocent was to find out who was behind setting him up.

When he got to the very funky house on Ninth Street in the Throgs Neck neighborhood in the Bronx, Terry wondered if he shouldn't have brought a baseball bat with him. The streets were filled with strange pieces of junk, like a rotten mattress with two rats peering out of the middle. And a gold-plated lamp which lay in the gutter. It was pretty well smashed to bits and looked as though someone had thrown it from a rooftop. third-

Probably in the middle of a fight or a murder.

He sucked in his breath and walked up the battered steps to her stoop, then hit the button to her fourth-floor walkup.

No one answered.

Maybe he should have called her first, after all. But if he had and she was guilty it would give her a chance to prepare an alibi or just run out altogether.

He tried another button. Again, nothing. Finally, he tried a third residence and there was a hoarse answer.

"Who is it?"

"Tommy Rodriguez," Terry said. "Rosalie's cousin. I'm just here to drop off a package. I think her buzzer is dead."

The front door buzzer went off and he was in.

He walked up the steps to the fourth floor, stepping over trash, and a child's broken G.I. Joe doll. Joe's left arm was missing, and he seemed to be looking down at it in a confused way. Like he was in shock he had come back to America and ended up here.

Terry knocked on Rosalie's battered metal door and it swerved open, making a creaking sound as it revealed the shattered apartment inside.

"Rosalie Torres?" he called. "It's Terry Brennan."

Nothing but silence.

He walked down the short hallway into the living room and immediately wished he hadn't left the gun with Kathy.

The cheap, ugly peach colored couch was turned on its side and ripped open. The stuffing was pulled out of it, lay strewn across the floor.

Same with the blue armchair across the room. Someone had cut the back of it in half with a knife and gone through it, looking for...what? The money, the stolen coke?

Did they find either of them?

He began to feel dizzy and slightly sick. Not due to the destroyed décor of the living room but from the smell he had just started to notice, which came from a back room. He went out into the hall again and headed toward the bedrooms.

He didn't have to travel far. Rosalie Torres was lying over the double bed on her back. Her throat was cut from ear to ear.

Her eyes were wide open and he thought they looked like they had been dead forever. There was no trace of the happy, witty girl who had been Joey's wife.

He recalled how her eyes had sparkled and danced as she spoke. She loved being alive and her eyes told the story.

Now they were lusterless, like two cheap buttons. Her mouth was open too, in a permanent scream.

The room smelled of shit and blood and he felt himself getting dizzier. He leaned against the bedroom door and tried to breathe. He sucked in air, but it was the air of death. He had to get the window open. Too late, it occurred to him that he shouldn't touch anything.

He turned to go back into the living room. He had to think, plan, but first he had to start to breathe again. Before he passed out.

He staggered against the door, but as he looked up to gather himself, he felt a tremendous blow to his jaw and he fell backwards, down to one knee in the hallway.

"You son of bitch," came a hoarse, European accented voice.

He tried to get up, but he was again on the end of a punch and he fell backwards, against the wall.

"You killed Rosalie, bastard."

He was able to see the man now. A thick necked, heavy lidded man with prominent cheekbones and a thick nose.

The man started to kick him again, but Terry reached out and grabbed his leg and jerked it upward. The man fell backwards himself and now, suddenly, they were facing one another, both of them on their butts in the hallway.

Robert Ward

"Hold it," Terry said. "I didn't kill Rosalie. I came up here to get her help finding out who killed Joey Gardello."

"Who are you?"

"Terry..."

"I see you somewhere. Wait, on paper. On front page. You are man police look for, no?"

"Yeah, but I'm not the killer. I'm a writer."

The man got up and dusted himself off. He completely ignored Terry's denial.

"So you kill Joey for drugs and now you come up here for what?"

"I didn't kill him for his drugs," Terry said. "Think of it. If I had his drugs and his money, would I come see his ex?"

"Maybe you wanted her next!"

The man reached down behind him and picked up a mop.

"Do not try nothing, 'cause I know how to use this!"

In spite of everything, Terry had to laugh.

"You know how to use a freaking mop?"

"You won't be laughing when I crack your head with it. In my hands mop is like lance."

"I see," Terry said. "Well, I'll make a deal with you, Sir Mopalot. I won't try anything violent if you don't."

"I don't know I can trust you," the man said, holding his mop in a menacing manner.

They seemed to be at a standoff. Terry slowly got to his feet and rubbed his jaw. The man with the mop looked at him in a curious manner.

"I am Johnny from Albania," he said. "I work as janitor in the building. Rosalie and me are great friends. I found her just before you come in."

"Then you know I couldn't have done it," Terry said.

"I don't know who done it," Johnny said. "All I know is she was dead when I come in to fix her kitchen light. You could maybe have kilt her then come back to get something you forget. They say murderer always returns to scene of the crime."

"Who says that?" Terry said.

Johnny looked at him as if he was appraising his words.

"Okay. Its dumb saying. I heard it on *Perry Mason*."

"Look, somebody killed Joey and Ray," Terry said. "Probably for their coke and money. Then they figured Rosalie must know, you see? Somehow she found out who did it. So now they killed her. Maybe they have the coke and the money and maybe not."

"I hear you clear and loud," Johnny from Albania said.

"Loud and clear," Terry said.

"What?"

"Nothing. The thing is, they were obviously looking for something, the way they ripped up the couch and chairs."

"And mattress too," Johnny said, looking into the bedroom.

Terry looked into the apartment. He had been so shocked by Rosalie's corpse he hadn't even noticed the torn-up mattress.

"Hmm. Could still be here," Johnny said.

"You want to help me look?"

"Yes. I can do that. We may be too late, though."

"Yeah, and there's one other thing," Terry said.

"Is?"

"Is, I have guys chasing me."

"How many guys?"

"Lots of guys. Cop type guys and drug dealer type guys.

Nicky Baines-type guys. They think I have the coke."

"So we have to hurry."

"Not that I don't appreciate it, but exactly why are you helping me?"

"I don't know. I love Rosalie. And you don't seem like criminal to me. I know many criminals in Albania, and more in Alaska. I even met criminals in New Jersey. They are all tougher than you. You seem like nice guy."

"That's it?"

"Yeah. That's it. That and I hate being a fucking janitor. I figure this is much more exciting."

"You're not afraid?"

"Oh yeah. I'm afraid. But, well, I knew a woman once. She needed help and I dint give it to her."

"Was she…"

"Yes. Kilt. Dead. Forever. 'Cause of me. Now let's start looking before those shitheads get here."

They tore up the place, riffling through the CD's, the paperback books, the back of the toilet, and the insides of all the kitchen drawers. They looked in the ceilings for loose tiles, and they pulled up the rugs. They found nothing.

"I don't think she has the coke," Terry said, slumping down on a kitchen chair. "Or they got it. Shit."

"It is massive frustrating," Johnny said. "Who else did Joey know?"

"Many people but she was the only one he really trusted. Still, maybe he didn't trust her quite enough."

"This is a problem in Albania too," Johnny said. "No one can trust no one else. Police come down on people all the time."

Johnny gave a deep sigh and leaned on his mop.

"I just think of something," he said.

"What?"

"Rosalie had a key. Not her apartment key but another key. She was always nervous she would lose it. She said to me it was very valuable."

"A key. To what?"

"I don't know for sure. But maybe safe deposit box."

"Yeah, man, we might have to tear the ceiling out."

"Big job. I call my cousins. They are great ceiling destroyers."

"No way," Terry said. "We have to keep this thing between you and me. But where the fuck..."

Terry felt as though his head weighed a thousand pounds. A key. Christ, it could be anywhere.

He shook his head and, in frustration, slammed his hand down on the kitchen table. The table shook, and the cabinets across the room nearly toppled over.

And at that moment a small gray and white cat came out from under the cabinet. He looked at Terry as if he were not amused and trotted towards his litter box.

Johnny laughed.

"Maybe we could ask him," he said.

The cat began to rake the litter box with his claws.

"Maybe he can tell us after all," Terry said.

He got up from his chair, walked across the room and leaned down. The cat skittered away as Terry picked up the box.

He held it level above his head and looked underneath it.

There, taped to the bottom, was a key.

"That must be to the bank up the street," Johnny said. "I know she had account there."

"No, it's not a bank box. It's got AMB written on it."

"What is that?"

"It's a mailbox key. American Mailboxes. You know where their nearest store is?"

"Yeah. Two blocks away."

"Number 237. Let's go."

Johnny smiled.

"I love this. An adventure."

"You won't love it half as much if Nicky and his boys catch up with us. Trust me."

They headed out to the landing and down the steps.

CHAPTER TWENTY-ONE

"Drop that mop!" said a female voice.

On the second-floor landing both men turned around in shock.

"I mean it, mister. The mop. Drop it!"

Johnny did as he was ordered. The mop fell to the steps and slid down to the next landing.

"Kathy," Terry said. "Put down that gun."

But Kathy kept the .45 trained on Johnny.

"Who is this guy?" Kathy said.

"He's the building's janitor," Terry said. "He's helping us. By the way, I thought you went back to New Jersey."

"I started to but then I thought of you alone up here, with no weapons. I hate you, but I don't want you to have your throat slit. Unless I do it."

"Who is this crazy woman?" Johnny asked.

"Kathy Anderson, meet Johnny from Albania."

"Where the hell is Rosalie Torres?" Kathy said.

"She's upstairs taking a nap." Terry said.

"What?"

"A really long nap. The kind you don't wake up from."

Kathy's lovely mouth formed a perfect O. Then she turned her attention to Johnny.

"You trust this guy? How do you know he didn't do it?"

"Me?" Johnny said. "How do we know you dint kill her? You look like a killer to me."

"Is that right?"

"Yes. Your eyes have killer glint," Johnny said.

"Killer glint? Well, you better hope you are wrong, mister Johnny From Albania. 'Cause I'm holding the gun. You don't even have your fucking mop anymore."

"She talks from gutter, Terry. Is this woman you are in love with?"

"Yeah, I'm afraid so. Look Kathy, Johnny is a good dude. He's helping us."

"That's very reassuring," Kathy said. "Do you always take the word of mop carrying thugs from a country of crazed killers?"

"You say one more nasty word on my country, and I will call my cousins. They are big, ugly bullymen, unlike me."

"He's okay," Terry said.

"And you know this, how?"

"I know it in my gut," Terry said. "Now you two shake hands. We're on the same side."

Kathy hesitated but eventually put her non-gun hand out to shake Johnny's. But he shook his head.

"I am no thug. I resent you and wonder if you were not responsible for the dead state Rosalie is in."

"And you called me crazy?"

"I need my mop. Can I please go down and get it?"

"Go ahead," Kathy said. "But don't try anything funny with it. Where are you guys going anyway?"

"To open a mailbox." He held up the key.

"I see," Kathy said.

She smiled at Terry in a lethal way and they all went

down the stairs. At the bottom Johnny was about to put his mop in the janitor's closet, when his boss, a black woman who wore a strange orange Afro wig and bright purple lipstick, stepped out of the elevator.

"Hey, Johnny. You know there's a mess inna basement," she said. "Busted sewage pipe. You need to get down there right now."

She walked by them in a queenly manner and went out to the street.

"Hell," Johnny said. "I always miss out on the fun."

"You're better off, bro," Terry said. "But thanks."

Johnny and Terry slapped five. Johnny started to do the same move with Kathy, but she showed him the gun barrel instead.

He shook his head and headed down the cellar steps.

"You need help, you can call me sometimes. I know many peoples who used to be wrestlers in Albania."

"I'll remember that," Terry said.

"A good man," Terry said, as they left.

"Like you'd know," Kathy said.

Kathy and Terry opened the mailbox. Inside were some mailers and something else, a book of some kind.

Terry looked at the green loose-leaf notebook.

He opened it and read the first page.

"The Journal of Joseph Gardello, Film Director."

"At least he wasn't pretentious." Kathy said.

"Yeah, but pretentious or not, it might give us a clue to who has the money and the coke."

"Let's go somewhere nice and dark and read it," Kathy said. "I mean before the cops or the drug dealers come and kill us both."

"Yeah," Terry said, kissing her forehead before she could move away from him. "This is fun, right?"

It wasn't long before they found a dark bar called Price's Play Pen on Arthur Avenue. They collapsed into a cozy booth in the back, ordered a couple of beers. Terry took out Joey's journal, but before he opened it, he placed his hand on Kathy's.

"Listen," he said. "What happened the other night. That isn't me. I just got drunk and coked up and...hell..."

"Did you have sex with that model?" Kathy looked at him with a dark seriousness in her eyes.

"Nah. We kissed a little bit but it was only because we were so stoned. Nothing happened and then she went off with some Italian director."

Terry didn't bother to tell her about the little trip he'd made to her photo shoot. He wanted to keep on living a while longer.

"If we're going to be together, Terry," she said. "It's got to be serious. I have strong feelings for you. But I've had enough experiences with assholes in my life. If you fuck around on me, or if you lie to me, I'm gone."

Terry leaned over and pulled her across the table and they kissed. He missed her lips and kissed her chin, but it was still passionate.

Then he opened Joey's journal.

"Let me come over there," Kathy said.

"Please," he said.

She scooted over to his side and they began to examine the book.

The dated entries seemed to fall into five types. Notes on:

1. Women Joey had met and thought he could score with. There were quite a few of them. Terry even knew some of them. He laughed at the fifth name down: Julie Christie. Beside her name was written a short paragraph assessing his chances. "Julie is a superstar but she has never met a real man from the streets like myself. She told me just last week that she was looking for somebody different than the usual glam boy actors, a real man who knew how to take care of a woman. This is me." Kathy cracked up. "Yeah," she said. "Julie couldn't make it without having a scummy junky in her life. It's so sad he died before he ever got to show her what a man he was."

2. Ideas about movies he could make, mostly horror films because they were the easiest to finance.

3. Personal notes...notes on Thaddeus...which said how resentful Joey was now that Thaddeus was too busy to see him.

4. Odd notes in the very back of the book. Notes under the heading Expansion, which read: "Expansion: Think of people who can be partners. People I can consign drugs to, for a percentage. NOT DRUGGIE TYPES, but smart people who will sell the shit to a small, select group of their own friends. Independent film makers from NYU, some artists, from Puffy's bar, not the Odeon which is too obvious. Maybe the crowd who hangs at the Ear and the other artist bar, Fanelli's."

5. Payments: J.W. and H.F. want their piece. Stall until the big deal comes through.

Terry was astonished.

"You know who this is, right?"

"Yeah. Jim Walker and Howard Freeman. They must have invested in Joey's business."

"That's right," Kathy said. "And that makes both of them possible suspects."

"Jesus. No wonder Walker wanted me out. He's trying to create distance from anyone even associated with Joey."

"What? I thought you told me he was so eager to assign you another piece. Terry...you are such a liar."

Terry felt his insides turn.

"I'm so sorry. I was desperate. I didn't want you to think I was a loser."

"I only think you're a loser when you lie. I'm giving you a pass on this but no more. Now what the hell are we going to do with Joey's journal?"

"I don't know. But we do have to get it to a safe place. If we get a safe deposit box it might keep us alive."

"Good idea," Kathy said. "Your first one, but what the hell? You need to start somewhere."

They headed out to the night, both exhausted. There was no way they could go back to either of their apartments in the Village, so they decided on a cheap hotel Terry knew on the Upper West Side.

"It's called the Franconia," Terry said. "Very charming dump."

"And how do you know it?"

"I know it because it was the place my hero Cornell Woolrich lived. I was amazed to find it's been re-opened."

Kathy put her arm through his.

"Did I do something right?" Terry asked.

"Yeah, you mentioned Cornell Woolrich. I love the movies they made from his stuff. *Deadline at Dawn*, *The Chase*, *The Window*, they're all wonderful. I'd love to act in one of those noir pictures."

Terry shook his head.

He hugged her and for about five seconds felt like the luckiest guy in New York.

He stopped, took her in his arms to kiss her, but suddenly heard a familiar voice behind them.

"Aww, isn't that cute?"

Jim Walker smiled in his snake like way and held a gun on them.

"Sorry, to interrupt you two lovebirds, but we need to take a ride."

He motioned his .38 toward a green Mercury Capri, which was parked a few feet down the street.

"What the hell are you doing, Jim?"

"Just protecting my ass, as all bright people do," Walker said. "I knew you two would head up here to Rosalie's. Did she give you the journal?"

"Journal?" Kathy said.

"Very good," Walker said. "Big innocent eyes. The slightly higher almost kid-like voice. You might win a Tony someday, Kathy, and Terry might write the play, provided you two help me find Joey's journal. Get in the car. Now!"

Having no choice, Terry started to get in on the passenger side.

"No, you drive and, Kathy, you get in the back. Hurry."

CHAPTER TWENTY-TWO

Terry drove down the black streets, the crumbling buildings hanging over them like decayed and jagged teeth.

In the back, Kathy had the journal tucked under her blouse.

"Where to?"

"Down to the next block and turn right."

"Looking for a dark alley?" Terry said. "Are you insane, Jim? What the fuck are you doing?"

"You really want to know, Ter? Fine. Joey told me he had a journal. He also told me there were several very compromising items in his journal about me. I was hard up. Had started gambling heavily. Maybe I shouldn't call it gambling, though. Gambling means you have a chance to win. The way I play cards, there's no gambling involved. I lost and then I lost some more and then I doubled down on my hands just so I could lose again. But Joey told me there was a way out. If I invested with him in his highly lucrative dope biz, I could recoup all I lost in no time. I gave him everything I had left. It worked for a while, too. He gave me my monthly payments right on time. I was starting to come back. But it was slow...I needed more money. You know how it is, Terry. You don't hang in Elaine's and date models unless you have money."

"Which models?" Terry said, trying to keep him talking.

"You don't know? Valerie Stevenson, my friend. And she's the kind of girl who likes nice people, nice places and nice things. She isn't going to hang long with an editor unless he's got some bread."

Kathy gave Terry an I-told-you-so look.

"So you invested more with Joey," Kathy said from the back seat.

"That's right. All I had and I took a loan out for more. That was Joey's idea. He had this plan, he said. It was going to be big, make both of us rich."

"What kind of plan?"

"Steal coke and start a bigger business. He needed someone to help him with the robbery."

"You stole from Nicky Baines?" Terry said. "Are you out of your mind?"

"I guess I was. I didn't have to do much. Just lie down in the road like I'd been hit by a car. The truck drivers stopped and a couple more guys hit them from the back. It went easy."

"They saw your face?"

"No. We never let the drivers out of the car. I got up and walked into the woods. It was so easy. There was so much coke. And there was so much money, too. That was a real surprise."

"Great. What happened then? Let me guess. You and Joey had a falling out. So you killed him and Ray, stole all the coke and decided to pin the whole thing on me."

Walker smiled.

"Wrong again. Turn here, Terry. We're going to go somewhere very nice and dark and I'm going to search both of you for that journal."

Terry started to turn but saw a dark one-way street which led to an even darker loading dock. He could already see how it was going to go down. Walker grabs the journal from Kathy, then kills them both. The cops would assume they'd been killed by Nicky Baines.

He turned the wheel slightly, so that the car was heading right toward the steel loading dock, which protruded out from the warehouse. Then he jammed his foot down on the accelerator.

"What are you doing, Brennan?"

Terry said nothing but drove faster. He watched the accelerator go from fifteen, to twenty to thirty and then fifty in six seconds.

"Terry," Kathy said.

"Get down, Kathy," Terry said.

She tucked herself in between the back seat and the driver's seat.

"Isn't this fun, Jim?"

"Stop, you crazy bastard. I'll fucking kill you."

"You can't. I'm going to kill myself, Jimbo. You know all of us writers are suicidal."

"Stop...stop...Now. I swear, I'll..."

Walker's eyes were wide open with fear. The loading dock was only seconds away.

"You fucker," Walker said.

He turned to look at the door.

"Give me the gun and I'll hit the brakes," Terry said.

"No!"

"Oh yes."

Walker's mouth hung open. He tried to speak but only sounds came out.

Only a hundred feet away, Terry slammed on the

brakes and drove the car into the dock on Walker's side. The steel dock slammed into the passenger side, and sheared off the right headlight, then buckled into the door. Walker threw himself toward Terry, and the gun went off.

Terry turned the wheel hard left and the car spun madly around in the loading area before coming to rest next to a dumpster.

Terry looked down at Jim Walker. The bullet had missed him and blasted a hole in the ceiling.

Kathy arose from the back seat, swallowing hard and staring at Terry as though he were a total stranger.

"You okay?" Terry said, as he picked up the gun.

"I'm fine. But Walker?"

Walker was lying in a heap on the floor. He looked up at Terry sheepishly and shook his head.

"Shit, man. I didn't mean it. I didn't know what I was doing?"

"How about when you killed Joey and Ray? You know what you were doing then?"

Walker was shaking as she sat upright.

"I didn't do it. I thought about it. I don't think I could have gone through with it, anyway. But someone beat me to it."

"Who?" Terry said.

"I don't know. You need to talk to someone who Joey trusted. Who was inside with him? Even though I gave him money, he never let me know what he was thinking."

"Fine, who might that be?"

"The person who knew him best? Thaddeus. He doesn't do coke, but his good friend Gina does. She has plenty of inherited money, and she's spent a lot on Joey's coke for her little parties."

Terry was shocked.

"Parties? She has a bunch of poets over her place."

Walker managed to laugh, as he straightened his shirt.

"Poets? That's a code word, my friend. You remember that night we were at your place and she borrowed that book from you?"

Terry looked at Kathy.

"Yeah, I do. She borrowed *The Story of O*. She said she needed it for some review she was writing."

"No, no," Walker said. "No review. That's her bible. She's into S&M big time. She uses the coke to arouse her guests."

Terry and Kathy looked at one another in shock. Gina—sweet, ironic, little Gina—was a Mistress of Pain?

"He trusted her. Told her his ideas."

Terry thought of the entry in the journal.

"But why would she be involved in stealing his coke?"

"Because she invested heavily, too, and he didn't come across with the money he owed her. There were two or three other people who had given him money, Howard Freeman and your agent, Barry Landsman."

"What?"

"Oh yeah, you didn't know that? He was involved in the little S&M parties, too."

"Jesus Christ," Terry said.

"You think Gina might know who whacked him?"

"It's a possibility. She might even have some of the coke."

"Who else was involved in the robbery?"

"At least two others. But I never saw them without their masks. Big guys though. Tough."

"Detectives Lazenby and Green," Terry said. "Count on it."

"Maybe," Walker said. "Listen, I have to know. Do you guys have the journal?"

"Could be," Terry said.

"Cute. Tell me. Am I in it?"

"Yeah," Kathy said. "Big time. And if anything happens to either one of us the journal goes to the *New York Times*. Asshole."

"Get out," Terry said.

"What do you mean? Out here in the Bronx? This is my fucking ride."

"Not anymore. Get the fuck out, Jim. We can't use you anymore, asshole. 'Cause you're kinda dead around here."

He aimed the pistol at Walker, who almost fell out the door.

"You fuckers. You're going to be so sorry for this."

Terry waved goodbye to him with his middle finger and started backing up as Kathy climbed into the front seat.

"Now we both have guns," she said. "Try not to kill me, okay?"

"Deal," Terry said.

"You know, I kind of like the bullet hole in the ceiling," Kathy said.

"Me too," Terry said. "Gives this piece of shit some class."

CHAPTER TWENTY-THREE

Clarence stood among the weeds at his uncle's place just outside of Caldwell. His Uncle Lou was hardly ever around anymore. He'd inherited some money and spent his time travelling around the world. Clarence took care of his place for him, and sometimes slept there over the weekends. Having a second place made him feel better about himself. He had fantasies that he'd bring his fellow mail carrier, Darlene Blaha, out for a romantic country weekend. But first he'd have to cut the weeds and clean the place up a bit.

But cleaning up wasn't what was on his mind today.

He'd recently read all about that journalist Terry Brennan from Elaine's. Wanted for drug dealing and a person of interest in a triple murder.

Terry Brennan from Elaine's. Oh Jesus Christ. It was like fate was enticing him to ready himself to come to the rescue of Thaddeus Bryant.

Okay, it was true that none of the articles he'd read on the paper or seen on the television had actually said Thaddeus was in danger but come on! How obvious was it, after all?

Brennan had stolen money and dope from Thaddeus' former best-friend Joe Gardello, and then killed both Joey and Ray when they threatened to strike back against him. On top of that the police had found the body of Rosalie Torres, Joey's ex-wife. Obviously, she threatened Terry, too, so she had to go!

And now, in a few days, the premiere of Thaddeus' movie *The Debt* would be playing and everyone who hung at the bar at Elaine's knew the score. A huge after-party at Elaine's with the crème de la crème of New York and Hollywood invited.

Maybe the fugitive Terry Brennan wouldn't make an appearance, but something told Clarence that he'd be there.

And he'd probably be packing.

He wasn't sure what the beef between Thaddeus and Brennan was, but this was the obvious place for them to have it out.

Or maybe not? Maybe Terry wouldn't be there at all.

Or maybe he would.

Or maybe...

Clarence cursed himself for being stupid. He'd once seen a movie called *Charlie* in which Cliff Robertson played a stupid guy who takes some kind of drug and becomes super smart. He even falls in love with the female scientist who gave him the drug. But in the end the drug stops working and he goes back to being a dumbass again. People said stuff like "Its okay, 'cause he won't remember when he was smart and he'll be fine."

But that was so wrong!

When you're stupid you know you're stupid and you feel like everyone else knows you are too. You think everyone is taking advantage of you. You worry you're too stupid to get a cute girlfriend, and even if you do, you worry you're too stupid to keep her. You worry about money you put in the bank because you know that banks can fail. You worry that the bank is ripping you off by giving you a lousy return on your money, but when you're stupid you worry that if you put your money into stocks the clever guys on Wall Street will give you a good return for like three weeks to make you feel happy, stupid guy, but then take all your money and put it into their own numbered accounts in the Cayman Islands. You worry that your house will fall apart too, but when you're stupid you can't fix it yourself so you are easy prey for evil plumbers who will do funny things with your basement pipes and cause a flash flood when you use the toilet.

When you are stupid you are basically afraid of everything and everybody, which also makes you hate everything and everybody.

Clarence spun out of his stupid reverie with a little determination and grit. Now that he was hobnobbing with the celebs, he felt smarter.

He couldn't say for sure that Terry would show up at the after party but that's what should happen.

Though he wasn't sure why.

Forget that. He decided to believe that Terry would make an appearance and that he would be there to Save the Fucking Day.

Noble Clarence would be ready.

Ready with his Uncle's old Beretta 1951 series handgun. At the first sign of trouble he would spring into action and blast Terry Brennan into next Thursday!

Thaddeus would be forever grateful, as would all the celebs at Elaine's, and he would become part of the inner circle.

There was no doubt about it.

This was his time.

Now he steadied his grip and aimed at the target bullseye he'd pasted up on a half-finished retainer wall in his Uncle's weedy back yard.

He drew a deep breath and slowly squeezed off the trigger.

The gun kicked in his hand. He walked toward the wall and found the bullet had pierced the outer circle of the target.

He felt a surly anger flash through him but quickly took a deep breath and talked to himself in a soothing voice: "Calm down, Clarence. Rome wasn't built in a day, pal. By the time the party comes around you'll be ready, bud. You'll be ready and Terry Brennan won't even know you're coming. Plus, remember this above all else. You are not stupid. Well, you were, but you're not now. And will never be again."

He walked back to the fallen-down porch and turned around, then counted off once more.

"Five, four, three, two, one. Fire."

He missed the target and smashed a window in his uncle's tool shed.

No matter. He would press on. After all, only stupid people gave up.

CHAPTER TWENTY-FOUR

Terry and Kathy stood in Tompkins Square Park across the street from Gina's building on Avenue A. They hid behind a trash barrel while they watched her leave her place.

"Probably headed up town to meet Thaddeus at Elaine's," Terry said.

"But how do we know?"

"We don't. Which is why I go in and you stay out here with these."

He held up two flares.

"Where did you get those?"

"Found them in Walker's trunk. Very decent of him to leave them there for us."

"Yes, wasn't it?"

"Well, I better start out. If you get bored, you can do some climbing on the jungle gym."

"Very funny. Don't stay in there long. I'm passing out from exhaustion."

"Me too. I'll be quick."

"Do you know what it is you're looking for?"

"Not really. Coke. Piles of cash. Something that gives her away."

"Do you really think she could be involved? With killing Joey for drugs?"

"No, not really. But I would have never thought Howard would have betrayed me, that my editor was a murderer in training, or that my agent would set me up to hand me over to the cops, either. Each and every day I am learning more and more and more, you know?"

She laughed.

"Get going, you maniac."

He kissed her on the nose and took off across the street.

The old building was falling down, rickety, and right next door to a clothing store called Planet Fashions. Very East Village, most of the clothes in the window were capes and shiny gray space boots. Tripping clothes. Terry walked across the street and up to the front door. The outer door was unlocked. He squeezed into the narrow foyer and looked for the mailboxes. There it was, a fourth-floor walkup.

Great. Made it even tougher to escape if anyone came.

He took out his nail file. Years ago, one of his first magazine stories had been about a second-story man, Junior Morrison. Junior could break into just about any place in New York with only a nail file. He had taught his skills to Terry, who had delighted in learning them. But he had never imagined he would ever use them. As he twisted the file back and forth, he realized if he got caught, he could be blowing his journalism career for good.

But he had to know…

Seconds later the lock gave, and he started up the steps.

By the time he reached the top he was winded, his heart pounding.

He took out the nail file and started twisting again. It didn't take long.

* * *

He walked through Gina's living room, looking around.

But there were only a couple of Eames chairs and an old blue couch.

He went upstairs, looked in her bedroom. Old furniture from what looked like a thrift store. A nice double bed with a New England patchwork quilt on it.

This did not look like the lair of a secret cokehead murderess.

He opened her chest of drawers, hoping to find a diary stuffed away under her clothes or under garments.

But no such luck.

He walked into the hallway and found another door. This one was locked. Nail file time again. In a few seconds he was in.

And there it was, just as Walker had said it would be. A room pained black with all the accoutrements one would need to be The Mistress of Pain.

A black rubberized table in which cuff "restraints" were hanging from all four corners. A giant Wheel of Pain, which could be spun so that the person held on it was upside down. In a little black bucket, he found whips and short lashes.

Who the hell was Gina after all?

And worse, did Thaddeus know about this little hobby of hers? Did he take part in it?

Christ. He suddenly wished he hadn't come in here at all. He didn't want to know these things. Not about Thaddeus. His hero, his idol, was some kind of S&M freak?

None of it had anything to do with Joey, did it? Wasn't

Walker just sending them on a wild goose chase to keep suspicion from himself?

As he rifled through the drawers and the cabinets and ceiling panels, he reminded himself of the scenario that made the most sense.

Joey and his brother had stolen coke from Nicky Baines, the drug kingpin, and partnered with Gina, who was selling it to different clientele than they were and splitting the money in some fashion. To cover their tracks, they had dumped some of the coke and the money on Terry, notified the cops, and presto, the perfect fall guy.

Think only of that. Find the coke. Find the money and somehow give it back to Nicky and explain to him what had happened.

Find the goddamned coke and the money.

He headed out of the chamber of horrors and went back to her study. He had to really go through this place. Meaning, if there were locked drawers that he couldn't open he would just have to break them open.

Outside, the temperature had dropped, and Kathy was doing pull ups. She had done twenty-one. Still in great shape. Still a good actress. It would be a shame to die helping her insane boyfriend.

Yet, there was something wonderful about him. She could feel it in him.

Well, maybe it hadn't totally manifested itself as of yet, but it would. She knew it. First of all, he was a brilliant writer. All he needed to do was to escape being killed by the corrupt police and Nicky Baines and he and she would probably have a wonderful time together, living in witness protection.

Jesus Christ, was she insane?

She should break up with him at once and marry an accountant.

But she had already gone out with an accountant and it was no fun, especially around tax time.

On the other hand, this was rather too much fun.

And, then again...

Suddenly, she saw something across the street. A cab pulling up. And out of it stepped two people.

Two very familiar people.

Oh shit. Oh hell.

Oh good. They were walking down the street to the corner bodega to get something.

She had just enough time.

She looked at a flare.

Just tear it off and hold it away from your face.

Yes, that was a good idea. Having a flare go off in your face would definitely draw all the wrong kind of attention.

Terry walked around the desk, tried to open the middle drawer. But it was locked. One more time with the nail file. He was getting good at this. If none of this worked out, he might have a brilliant career as a second-story man.

Twist turn and presto. Seconds later it was open. There were some bills held secure by a rubber band on the left, and some contracts for articles written for the *Voice*. He looked beneath them. Not much...no, wait...

There was something there. A manila envelope. He

opened it quickly and pulled out its contents.

Photos. Rather old photos of Gina and Thaddeus. In two of them they were on the campus at Yale. In one of them they were standing together in front of the Sterling Memorial Library. Smiling. Thaddeus with his arm around Gina. Her face was turned toward his and her look was one of total adoration.

In another photo, they stood in front of the Yale art gallery. This time they were facing one another and were hugging one another happily. The smile on Gina's face was one of total abandon and worship.

The other photos were of Thaddeus. Here was Thaddeus smiling at Elaine's. Thaddeus in the Hamptons at the Steven Talkhouse. Thaddeus at Bobby Van's talking to Willie Morris and James Jones. Thaddeus walking in the Village, right across the street at Tompkins Square Park.

Thaddeus and Gina at Elaine's, the two of them at some Upper East Side bash talking to Al Pacino.

Well, there it was, what he had always expected. She idolized Thaddeus.

Would do anything for him.

The two of them into S&M? Well, if Thaddeus wanted to…of course she'd go along with him. What else didn't he know about them?

Terry felt sorry for her. As bright and attractive as she was, and to give her whole life to a man who couldn't love her. Poor Gina.

Then he reminded himself to stop wasting his sympathy. She might have set him up for murder.

Terry sat down in her desk chair and tried the drawer on the right. It, too, was locked, and it took him a while to get it open.

There was something inside. What seemed to be a big, thick manuscript. It was in a large mailer, so he took it out, carefully slid it out on the desk.

There was a blank piece of paper on the top. He slid it to the side and looked at the title.

And there was the surprise of his life. Something that made Gina's little Pain Pad upstairs seem small by comparison.

Not coke. Not money. Not a sex diary.

Instead, another kind of book. A book written on lined paper like the kind a schoolgirl uses.

A novel entitled *The Debt*.

And written beneath the title in a very small, neat hand were the words: "By Thaddeus Bryant."

CHAPTER TWENTY-FIVE

Though she was now freezing to death and totally exhausted and terrified that Thaddeus and Gina would come back any second, Kathy was rather proud of herself. She had set the flare off perfectly, it was glowing and shimmering and giving off sparks like crazy, and she was holding it over her head and bouncing up and down on her heels and doing everything short of screaming, "Terry, get the fuck out of there, will you?"

Only it was really kind of impossible to feel proud when all your efforts were totally fruitless. No one was looking down from the window.

No one was coming at all.

And now they were coming. Thaddeus and Gina with their shopping bag and their *New York Times* and they were going to walk in on him and oh God...somehow she had to let him know.

He sat at the desk in a daze. What in God's name was this? A copy of Thaddeus' best-selling novel, *The Debt*, written in Gina's handwriting? Could she have...but he couldn't finish the idea. It was too huge for him to take in.

He turned the pages, all written out in longhand. And there were the first words.

How much does anyone owe to the people in his past?

His mother and father and relatives, his so-called "best friends" of youth, his earliest lovers, that girl who drove him crazy in her short shorts and tank top down the street? This was a question which Max West often asked himself. And yet, no matter how hard he worked at it, the answer never came. Or it came with far too many conditional clauses. Sometimes, Max thought it would drive him crazy.

A brilliant, reflective opening passage, and one which takes the entire novel to answer.

Now, sitting here, Terry recalled himself reading that passage, sitting in the cozy back room of the Lion's Head on a Saturday afternoon. Kathy brought him Jack Daniels and he spent four hours sipping his whiskey and getting lost in Thaddeus Bryant's awesome first novel. He knew at that moment that he would have to do a piece on Bryant for some magazine, hopefully *Rolling Stone*, though they rarely profiled writers. But he could talk Jim Walker into it, he was sure, because this book took on all the adventures and moral dilemmas of their generation. Their flirtation with radicalism, their fight against the Vietnam War, Women's Liberation, ambition versus loyalty to the past. All the major themes which no one had successfully dealt with. And, by God, the author had brought it off. He had to know him, learn from him...

The writer was a genius. There was no other way to put it.

He read on, as Thaddeus' hero went to Vietnam, but once there, having seen the whole horrible fuck-up firsthand, he had come back and started a Veterans Against the War organization, for which he was pilloried by his ex-service buddies.

It was all there, just as it had been on the printed pages of the novel.

Brilliant, heartfelt, stylistically clever, it sounded the way Thaddeus talked. Christ, it *was* Thaddeus.

And yet, here it was, written out in Gina Wade's hand.

He tried to think of some reason Thaddeus's novel could be sitting in this desk, written in Gina's handwriting.

But no matter what he came up with, the answer was always the same.

Gina Wade must have written it and let Thaddeus claim it as his own.

No sooner had he told himself this than he found a page that was not the text but a note to Gina herself. And obviously from herself.

"Cut this part back. Thaddeus wants to keep the action taut. No excessive blather."

He went through the pages faster now and found more editorial notes.

"Make this love scene sexier. T. wants to make sure the novel has plenty of juice."

And again: "Battle scene not graphic enough. Thaddeus says people today want blood and plenty of it. I must remember T. is in competition with motion pictures, which now show everything. This isn't the fifties anymore!"

He knew he had to get up and get the hell out of there, but he felt welded to the spot.

Gina Wade had written *The Debt*, not Thaddeus Bryant.

It seemed impossible, but here it was. In front of him.

She had written it and he had put his name on it. But why? Money, for sure. He must have paid her enough to rent this place and put plenty in her bank account.

But that wasn't enough.

He remembered Thaddeus saying to him one night that Gina was the best student he'd ever had. That her writing was amazing, but she had a terrible problem with her own self-esteem. She was sure she was no good, would never be any good, that she was a second-rater. He had hired her as a researcher to help her gain confidence, to get used to being around the literary world. The hope, Thaddeus had said that whiskey-filled night, was that she would calm down, realize that she could do it. He was working with her, he'd said, teaching her how to string together narrative, to not only come up with a few nuggets of insight but to tell a longer, complex story with sub-plots and how to make those sub-plots run like a river into the ocean of the main plot.

And when Terry had asked him, how she was doing, Thaddeus had answered, "Much better. I mean, it's a slow process. She was battered and sexually molested by her father, though you must never tell anyone about this. There are days, weeks, when she can't bring herself to write a single word. But I'm sticking by her. Some day that girl is going to write a great novel. I swear it."

Which had made Terry admire his friend that much more.

How many great novelists would have time to take on a "reclamation project" like Gina? Didn't she sap his energy with her constant whining, crying, and black moods? Most writers were entirely selfish, and rightly so. There was nothing harder than writing, nothing in the world. To drag stories, characters, and entire fictional histories out of yourself was an exhausting, all-consuming task. No wonder so many writers wore down when they were young, lost themselves in drinking and drugs and sex. Anything not to face the blank white page. And yet, here was noble Thaddeus Bryant, All-American Novelist, taking on poor, pathetic Gina!

My God, the man was not only a great American novelist but a saint!

Terry felt a kind of full body blush come over him, an embarrassment that was so total it seemed to choke his windpipe.

God, he had been such a fool. He had admired, worshipped...oh, just say it, loved Thaddeus Bryant like the mentor, big brother, father he had never had.

And now he knew the truth. Thaddeus Bryant was a total fraud.

They were almost to the house. And she was running out of sparks. Of course, she had a second flare, but what was the point? What the hell was he doing up there?

They were walking up the steps, and any second they would be inside.

She threw down the flare and ran for Walker's car.

Terry was putting it together now. He could see it clearly.

Thaddeus would never be able to drag another novel out of Gina. No...now he could see it clearly. He'd end up in Hollywood. Take Gina with him where she'd be invaluable as a "story person." He'd make millions in the movie biz, with her help. And after that, well, there were always bright young things from USC who would fill Gina's shoes after he had planted her in the desert somewhere.

Terry laughed at himself. To think, he'd actually worried about Thaddeus' soul if his movie was a hit. What would happen to the sensitive artist once he got out there among the sharks? Would they eat him alive? Poor, poor Thaddeus!

Ha! What a horrible fucking joke. Thaddeus would devour *them* whole.

But still...what did any of this have to do with Joey's death?

Okay...think...

Joey had known Thaddeus his whole life. He must have had some inkling that Thaddeus couldn't write *The Debt.* Maybe...maybe he followed up his hunch and had found out the truth. Wait, what was it that Willie had told him the other night at Studio 54?

That Joey had told Willie that he was soon headed for something big, a really big score, after which he'd have it made.

Which could have only been that he was blackmailing Thaddeus...

That had to be it. Joey had put the squeeze on him for a large chunk of money. Or even worse, maybe he wanted Thaddeus to get *him* a movie deal? That would be all Thaddeus needed. A failed, big mouth creep from the Bronx tailing after him. Constantly looking over his shoulder.

He took out his Vig Minolta 116 camera and took a picture of the title page with Gina Wade's name on the front cover.

What the hell was that noise? Somebody was honking a car horn over and over. So irritating.

He kept clicking away, took pictures of the first sixteen pages...God knows what he would do with them but they were all he had for now. He had just clicked page seventeen when he figured out the honking sound.

He had forgotten to look out the window for the flare. Kathy was warning him with the horn. Idiot!

And now he could hear them coming up to the door. He recognized their voices at once.

Gina was fiddling with the lock and Thaddeus was saying, "Let me do that. Sometimes you're just all thumbs, Gina."

"I'm sorry, Thaddeus. I'm just so nervous these days."

Terry replaced the book in the desk and managed to re-lock it again. As he was leaving her study, he saw a purple amulet which Gina sometimes wore around her neck. It gave him an idea. Crazy, but then, he was crazy to still be here. He picked it up and placed it in his jacket pocket.

Then he slid his camera in his other pocket, and hurried into the hall, took a left into the tiny kitchen.

He quickly unlocked the kitchen window and pushed up hard. It wouldn't budge.

He heard them coming in the front door. Still chatting: "You have to keep your cool," Thaddeus said. "We're almost there, baby. Headed toward the West Coast and a giant deal with Twentieth."

"Am I included in that deal, Thaddeus?"

"What? You have to ask?"

"Just need a little reassurance. Especially when you're going to be out there having lunch in the commissary with all those beautiful young actresses."

"Gina," Thaddeus said. "You know none of those air-heads can hold a candle to you, baby. Hey, what was that?"

"That" was Terry pushing the kitchen window up so hard it gave a small squeak. He climbed out on the fire escape and looked down. No way he could get to the ground before Thaddeus came out and looked down at him.

He took the steps to the rooftop trying hard not to make much sound.

Behind him Thaddeus entered the kitchen and looked around.

"I didn't hear anything, honey," Gina said.

"Well, I did." He opened the window and looked out. "Was this window locked?" he said.

"I'm not sure. I sometimes forget about it."

"Well, you shouldn't do that, Gina. You should never leave this place unlocked. Never."

Thaddeus headed out to the fire escape himself. Looked around. Nothing. The roof? Had he heard something up there?

He quickly went up the fire escape steps and climbed to the tarpaper rooftop.

He looked east and west. Saw nothing but three chimneys.

He listened closely. Satisfied, went back down the fire escape to Gina's apartment.

Terry let out his breath and crumpled to the roof behind the second chimney.

He felt a chill pass through his body. Then he found a backfire escape and silently came down. When he came around the block Kathy was sitting on the curb, weeping.

"Kathy? What's wrong?"

She looked up and wiped away her tears.

"Oh, my boyfriend just got caught inside that house and they tied him up in some torture chamber and now he's dead and I was just starting to really like him. You asshole! Why didn't you look out the window? I was practically the statue of fucking liberty out there!"

He took her in his arms and held her close to him.

"You're right. I'm an idiot, alright. But let's get out of here now. Because I know what it's all about now."

"Is it bad?"

"Yeah," he said. "Bad. Really bad."

CHAPTER TWENTY-SIX

As they drove Walker's car across toward to the West Village, Terry told Kathy what he had discovered.

"Christ," she said. "I'm so sorry, Terry."

"How could I be such a sucker? They must have seen me coming. The innocent kid from the sticks."

She leaned over and squeezed his arm.

"Shut up. That's why I like you. You're only one half as hip as you think you should be. If you actually made it all the way to the Massively Hip level, you'd be a creep like Thaddeus."

He smiled and put his free arm around her.

"It just occurred to me. You shouldn't be with me. No one knows you're involved but Walker and he won't talk."

She looked at him and shook her head.

"Shut up, Terry. I'm in. Now turn down here."

"The next block?"

"Yeah. I know where we can go."

"Where?"

"Sha's place."

"Sha, the other waitress at the Head?"

"One and the same."

"How do you know she's home?"

"I don't. But she always leaves the key under her mat.

I've let her crash at my place many times. We both need some sleep before we pass out."

"You got that right," Terry said. "I love you, Kathy. I mean it."

"You're only saying that because I'm saving your life and I'm good with a gun."

"You're right," he said. "I'm afraid if I ditched you, you'd blast me."

She smiled and wrinkled her nose.

"Try it and see," she said.

Sha was a peroxide blonde with six cats. She was dressed in a blue slip and was smoking a giant blunt.

"Jesus," she said. "Get off the street. The cops, the gangsters, and the national guard are looking for you."

"Gangsters, too," Kathy said. "How exciting."

"I know," Sha said. "There was this giant black dude in the Head today. Named Alexander. He wanted to know all about you, Terry. And I didn't get the impression he was a reader."

"We won't stay long," Terry said. "We just have to get some sleep. But if that's not cool..."

"It's cool," Sha said. "You guys go lie in the back room. Just throw the clothes off the bed. I'm sorry it's a mess, but my boyfriend and his kids were here last night."

Kathy walked over and hugged Sha.

"Hey," Sha said. "The Head is family. Do you have your gun, Kathy?"

"We have two guns," Kathy said.

"Good, me too," Sha said.

"You have two guns?" Terry said.

"I didn't want 'em," Sha said. "But my mom is from Montana. She came into town and left them here for me. Birthday present. What are you gonna do?"

She handed Kathy the blunt, but Kathy turned it down.

"That shit makes me paranoid," she said. "And right now, we have enough real enemies. Let's get some sleep."

Kathy slept almost immediately after she hit the pillow. Terry looked down at her, at her long, black lashes, the curve of her mouth. He loved her nose, her wisps of hair by her ears, her forehead, her ears. Such nice ears. How had he ever thought of anyone else?

Why had he?

Then he remembered Thaddeus' Joan Blondell riff. So funny, so nasty. Was the idea to keep him close? So he could be easily found and easily arrested?

Or did he simply just enjoy fucking with people?

Perhaps that was what he did instead of love them.

The thought irritated him and suddenly, exhausted as he was, he felt awake. Wide awake.

Christ, what a mark he'd been. How could he have been so dumb?

He felt assaulted by shame. And then by fury. He would get even with Thaddeus. He'd bring him down, somehow.

Kathy stirred and he kissed her forehead and slid out of bed. The apartment was hot. The heat was oppressive, or maybe it was just the heat from his own embarrassment.

He had to get out of there, feel the air on the street for just a minute. It was risky but not all that dangerous. Not really.

No one would be out here on Eighteenth Street. He

could get some real air, just stop for a second. God, he was so damned tired.

Outside the air was as fresh as he had hoped. The moon shone down on the Village. He loved New York. If he ever got out of this, he would marry Kathy and they would live in the Village together and they would have kids and the kids would go to the Village Community School and it would be perfect.

Okay, not perfect. But good, a good life...

Forget all the star shit. Just be a good man and live a good life and...

"Hey. Look who it is?"

He turned and saw a very big black man holding a .38 automatic.

"Nicky Baines wants to have dinner with you, Brennan. So move it. 'Cause he hates it when his guests are late."

He shoved Terry toward the corner, where a black limo screeched to a stop. Terry started to turn and say something, but Alexander smashed him in the temple. He started to fall but felt strong arms catch him and throw him inside.

CHAPTER TWENTY-SEVEN

Alexander's fist swung in a smooth arc and connected with Terry's jaw, snapping his head back as he groaned in pain.

However, Terry was surprised to find that a louder scream came from Alexander than from himself.

"Mutherfucker, Jesus fucking Christ that hurt. I can't freaking believe it. Goddamn." He shook his right hand like he was doing some kind of strange jazz dance. "I 'bout broke my fucking hand."

His two massively muscled "assistants," Bo and Earle, who stood behind him in the midtown garage, had to turn away so that he wouldn't see them laughing.

Alexander stopped shaking his hand and gingerly touched the middle finger of his right hand with his left hand.

"Fucking cracked it on you. You gonna pay for that, Brennan."

Terry shook his head in a way that said he had given up hope. But he had to try again anyway.

"Look, I told you. I told you three times already. I didn't have anything to do with stealing Nicky Baines's drugs and money."

"You were friends with Joey Gardello, mutherfucker, and…"

Terry felt his head droop over to one side. He'd never

had a professional beating before. He'd understood from books that the good professional beating hurts but doesn't kill you. He really hoped that was true. On the other hand, he felt sort of like he wanted to die.

"Well?" Alexander screamed into his face. "You better tell me something fast!"

"Look, Joey and I weren't even real friends. I only knew him through Thaddeus Bryant."

"Bullshit. Know you had him down your place. You and him and your cohorts rob the truck and then you rob him. He finds out and you gotta kill him and his goofball brother."

"No," Terry said. "That's wrong. Look, this whole thing isn't even about drugs."

"What? You losing your mind, son?"

"No, I mean drugs were stolen by Joey. And his brother. Then Thaddeus stole some of the drugs from them and placed them in my locker to make it look like I was involved. Just like you think."

"Who the hell is Thaddeus?"

"A novelist," Terry said.

Alexander looked at him like he was speaking an alien language.

"What's some book writer got to do with all of this?"

"Because Joey was blackmailing him about something else."

It was weird. Even though he knew that Thaddeus hadn't written his novel and had probably set him up for murder he couldn't quite bring himself to say it out loud. Some loyal part of him still hoped that he had come to the wrong conclusion, that there was some logical, sensible way that Thaddeus could explain why Gina had written his whole novel in her handwriting. Then they could go on as before with Thaddeus being the big brother he'd never had, and be the happy, aspiring, and talented little brother. Not to mention Gina as his little sister. One big happy family of artists, instead of cheap, lying hustlers who would do anything or kill anyone to get ahead.

Alexander had walked away from him for a few seconds, but now he was coming back.

His face wasn't twisted in anger or fury. Rather, his eyes were confused and imploring.

"What you saying is Joey and his brother wasn't killed by you 'cause you stole his dope and he was coming after you, but by this Thaddeus novelist guy who was being blackmailed by Joey."

"Exactly," Terry said. "That's right."

"But what 'bout the dope and money in your locker?"

"Thaddeus planted them there to make me look guilty of three murders."

"And this book writer, he really killed 'em all."

"No, he had somebody else do it. I think."

"Who?"

"I don't know."

But then it occurred to him. How did the two cops Lazenby and Green know to come to his pad right after Joey was killed? Who told them to? Thaddeus, of course.

And who was most likely to shoot Joey and Ray?

They were. Probably to get a piece of Thaddeus' Hollywood deal. Super high paid technical assistants and story consultants. Of course. He told Alexander what he thought. Bo and Earle looked shocked.

"Lazenby and Green?" Earle said. "But we know those dudes real well. They even do stuff for us…"

Earle never finished his sentence, as Alexander hit him with the back of his hand in the chops.

"You should shut the fuck up. We don't tell our business to no one."

Earle, his mouth bleeding, nodded assent. Then Alexander turned back to Terry.

"That's a good story," Alexander said. "But that's all it is. A freaking story. If it's true, you tell me where the cocaine that went missing is."

"I don't know," Terry said. "I was looking for it myself. Until you caught me."

"And what was you gonna do with it? Sell it back to us?"

Earle and Bo cracked up and high fived one another.

"Nope," Terry said. "Give it back to you."

"Sheeet," Earle said. "You not only a lying sack of shit, you a fool too."

Bo nearly fell out laughing.

But Alexander was not amused.

"You two clowns shut the fuck up. You 'spect me to believe that you was gonna find the dope, walk it over here, and, what, present it to Nicky?"

"I might have taken a cab," Terry said. "But, yes, that was my idea."

"Just like that."

Alexander started untying Terry's bonds.

"You letting me go?" Terry said, in a hopeful way.

"No, I taking you on a little tour. I want you to see somebody. Another person who tells stories."

The two thugs held his arms as they pushed him forward behind Alexander. They went down a dark corridor, at the end of which Alexander turned on the lights.

There was a dark room with a Plexiglas window in the middle of the door. Alexander used a key on his ring to open it.

Once inside they turned on the room light.

Terry wished they hadn't.

Lying on a bloodstained cot on the far side of the room was a beaten and moaning Willie Hudson.

"Christ," Terry said. He tried to run to him, but Earle and Bo held him tight.

"Terry," Willie said.

He coughed and spat up blood, which dribbled down his shirt front.

"Why?" Terry said to Alexander. "He didn't do any-thing."

"Bullshit," Alexander said. "He a friend of young Joey. They go way back. He know everything that man do. He knows and he gonna tell or he ain't gonna be breathing for too long."

Willie tried to sit up. But his ribs were broken and when he turned even a half inch the pain shot from his side, up into his shoulders, and into his temples.

"They want me to say you was involved. But I wouldn't."

Terry felt a violent rage coming over him. Which sur-prised him. The fear he had felt only minutes before in the hallway had been subsumed by his anger.

"Willie doesn't know anything. Look how bad you've beaten him. If he knew anything at all don't you think he'd have told you guys by now?"

"We don't know for sure. Willie is a tough guy. He can take beatings of all kinds. But you a writer. We doubt you that tough. We think you gonna tell us anything we want to know after only say another hour of, uh...Advanced Aggressions. You dig?"

Terry didn't say anything at all. He dug though. All too well.

Earle and Bo turned him around violently and they headed out of Willie's room and back down the hall for another tutorial.

CHAPTER TWENTY-EIGHT

Bo and Earle brought Willie out of his bloody bed and laid him down on the floor next to Terry. Alexander walked over to the electric welder, a long, black prong with a sharp point at the business end. He picked it up and plugged it into the wall outlet. It began to throb and light up in a nasty manner. Then he looked at Terry and smiled.

"Here's the deal. I said it once and I'm gonna say it again. One last time. You cop to it and we going to kill you nice and fast. Toss you in the river. But you play with me, you get the drill. Now, I know for a fact you, Joey, and Willie took the money from one of Nicky's trucks. Then you turned round and re-stole it from them. Which is why it was in your apartment locker. Then you wasted them so they couldn't revenge themselves on you. Only thing that makes sense."

"Oh yeah," Terry said. "That makes perfect sense. Then after I killed them both, I called the police on myself and had the cops come raid my storage unit and bust me. Also, I came home when they were there so they could find me easier. You're a fucking genius. You should get your application into the NYPD today!"

Bo and Earle couldn't keep it in any longer. They both snort-laughed and slapped five.

Which irritated their boss in the extreme. Alexander turned on them.

"You two assholes think that is funny?"

"Well, shit," Bo said. "It was *kinda* funny."

"You say that one more time I am gonna take Big Electric Baby here and stick it up your asses just to warm it up."

"Gotcha," Bo said. "That shit wasn't funny at all."

"No way, boss. Unfunny as hell."

Alexander started to wave the red-hot welder in front of Terry.

"The only question now is which of you two clowns will use the Big Boy on Terry first?"

Terry tried to keep his cool but felt his sphincter muscle curl up inside him.

From up above them, on a small porch which led to his office, came a sudden voice. A voice which made all of them church quiet.

"What the fuck is going on down there?"

Alexander felt his Adam's apple get as large as a softball which had laid out on a soppy field.

"Questioning these fucking thieves, Nick," Alexander said.

He started a silent prayer that Nicky would accept that explanation and let him do his work.

But Nicky was walking down the steps now. Slowly, softly, like a panther.

He was wearing a green silk ascot and a houndstooth jacket. Alexander remembered he was going to an important dog show. He walked toward Alexander, shaking his head.

"They tell you anything useful yet?"

"Ah, not yet," said Alexander. "But I'm going to use

some more persuasive techniques." He waved the electric welder around.

Nicky wasn't impressed.

"Put that thing down."

He turned toward Terry.

"You the writer? For *Rolling Stone*?"

"That's me," Terry said.

"Hmmm," Nicky said. "You ever pull any heists?"

"I stole a Blackhawk Comic from the Read's Drug Store once when I was a kid."

Nicky laughed.

"I used to love that comic. What was that guy in the gang, the little Chinese guy?"

"Chop Chop," Terry said.

"Chop Chop, that's right," Nicky said. "I loved that fucking guy."

Terry had to laugh. The absurdity of being tied up by Harlem's biggest gangster and discussing Blackhawk Comics was almost too much to take.

Nicky stopped laughing and leaned in on Terry.

"I heard everything you said from my listening post upstairs. You think this writer guy, Thaddeus, is involved in all this? Did he help steal the dope and the money?"

"I don't think so," Terry said. "I think he learned about it from Joey and then took advantage of the situation."

"And how did he get shit get in your locker?"

"I'm not sure. But through a mutual friend. And I'm not at all sure that was your coke. I'm guessing he bought some of the stolen coke and used it and some of his own money to set me up."

"But why would he do that? He got something against you?"

Terry sighed and shook his head.

"No, nothing. After he had Joey, Ray and Rosalie killed, he needed someone to take the rap. I was the perfect patsy."

Nicky sighed.

"And this guy Willie here? How's he involved?"

"I think he helped take off the truck with Joey and Ray." Alexander said.

Willie slowly looked up from his chair.

"What day did the robbery happen?"

"January 15th," Nicky said.

"Well, you check it out. I had that day off and I spent the night down at The Bowery Church helping out Father Greer."

"Oh bullshit," Alexander said. "Now you coming on like some Mother Teresa? That's good."

"No, I ain't no saint," Willie said. "But he helped me when I was down and out, and I spend two days every month helping him feed the street people down there. Call him and ask him if you want."

"Sheeet," Alexander said. "I'm gonna fuck you up some more and then we will get the real story out of you, Saint Willie."

He moved toward Willie, but Nicky stopped him.

"I believe him," he said. "He dint do it."

He turned toward Terry.

"But you I'm not so sure of."

"If you let me and Willy out of here, I think I can prove it."

"Don't believe him, boss," Alexander said. "He just making up a story. That's what these writer mutherfuckers do, man. They make up shit and get your head all turned around."

Terry waited, holding his breath. He could barely believe he'd had the nerve to say all this stuff to Nicky Baines. But, then again, he'd always been cool under fire as a journalist.

Nicky was walking over to the now glowing electric drill. He pulled it out of the wall and walked toward Terry.

"This here baby makes people talk and talk...well, in between screams, that is."

Terry tried to swallow but his mouth was bone dry.

Nicky held the horrible glowing prong close to Terry's face. The heat coming off it felt as though it was melting his eyebrows.

"You telling me the truth?"

"I am," Terry said.

Nicky nodded and put the drill down on a steel table.

"I'm gonna let you and your friend go. He's off the hook. But you are still on it, you understand? You got two days. You ain't back with proof that this writer asshole did it, then you and old Daisy here will have a serious ass meeting. You dig?"

"I dig," Terry said.

"But, boss," Alexander said. "He's the one. Him and Willie here."

"Shut up, A. You heard what I said. Release them both. And give 'em a ride to wherever they want to go."

A few minutes later Terry almost had to pinch himself to believe that:

1. He had almost been executed in a most unappealing way and

2. He and Willie Hudson were now in the world's most dangerous criminal's cushy limo being driven downtown by one of Nicky's drivers, dressed in full livery.

As they rode along, Willie Hudson looked over at him. The bulletproof shield was up, so they could talk.

"You said Joey was blackmailing Thaddeus. What the hell was that about?"

"I don't want to say just yet. But, trust me, it's true."

"Son of a bitch," Willie said. "The great Thaddeus. Joey worshipped him."

"I know. But once he found out what his idol had done, he really had him."

"Makes sense."

"Yeah. But I'm only ninety-nine percent sure. I gotta talk to Thaddeus."

"How you gonna do that?"

"Very carefully."

Willie looked thoughtful.

"You got to come at him like you don't know nothing and wear a wire. Get him to talk about it."

"Great idea, man. Is there any way you could get me something like that? They must have tech stuff at Studio 54."

Willie turned away from Terry. He remembered telling Green and Lazenby that Terry might be their man. He felt lousy about it now. But not dumb-lousy.

"Hey, man, you seem like good people to me, Terry, but I can't get into nothing like that. I borrow mikes and tape stuff and they find out, I get fired and lose everything."

Terry sighed.

"How about you do it because I just saved your ass in there?"

But Willie wouldn't relent.

"Hey, you can see it that way. I see it like you got me involved in something that got my ass beaten half to death, something I had nothing to do with. Know what I mean?"

"I guess I do."

The limo pulled up across the street from Studio 54. Rollerina was skating back and forth in front of the entrance, dressed like Alice. She looked at their limo, her eyes slitting as she tried to see through the tinted glass, then zoomed off, as another limo parked behind them.

Willie half opened the back door, then turned and looked at Terry.

"Good luck, Terry," Willie said. "I wish I could help you, baby, But I kind of quit being a martyr right after they killed Martin. And I'm too old to start up again."

"I dig," Terry said. "Take it easy, Willie. And thanks for the help you did give me."

Willie nodded slowly, got out, and headed into the back door to work. Terry hoped he might change his mind at the last minute like people do in movies when they're hit with pangs of conscience.

But there was no last-minute reprieve. Willie went inside, the door closed behind him and Terry was on his own.

CHAPTER TWENTY-NINE

On Sunday, Terry sat at Sha's apartment with a calico cat on his lap and the phone in his hand.

The phone rang a few times, then Thaddeus answered.

"Hi, Thaddeus."

"Terry! Thank God. Where the hell are you? The cops have been here and everyone in New York is looking for you."

"I know," Terry said. "I think we need to talk, Thaddeus. Do you know where The Bells of Hell is?"

"Yeah, sure."

"Meet me there in forty minutes, Thaddeus. And come alone. If there are any cops you'll regret it."

There was a long silence.

"Terry, what is this, some kind of joke? Why would I bring any cops? I'm on your side, man."

"Good," Terry said. "Then you don't have a thing to worry about."

He hung up and looked at Kathy, who was petting an orange cat named Alfie.

"You going to take one of the guns with you?" she said.

"Yeah," Terry said. "I am. Now show me how to use that safety again, will you?"

* * *

The Bells of Hell was a punk hangout at Thirteenth and Sixth. The place smelled of moldy bread and dog piss, though Terry had never seen a dog anywhere near the place. As he entered, he saw the rock critic Lester Bangs holding forth to a small group of admirers. Standing with him but looking bored was Richard Hell, this season's star attraction at CBGB's.

Thaddeus sat in a dark booth in a darker corner. As Terry reached the booth Thaddeus offered him his hand. Without standing.

"There you are! At last. Where have you been? Look at your face. What happened to you?"

"I walked into a forearm."

"You should get someone to look at that."

"No, I like it this way. Reminds me of what a sap I've been."

"But what happened?" Thaddeus said, his voice aching with concern.

"I had some interesting talks with Nicky Baines."

Thaddeus' voice rose as he spoke: "You were with Nicky? Just now?"

"Yeah, that's right, "Terry said. "Surprised he let me go? Sorry, but we got along fine. We're even thinking of starting a publishing company together."

Thaddeus managed a laugh.

"What did you two book lovers talk about?"

"Just told him the truth. That I had nothing to do with robbing his dope or killing Joey, Ray or Rosalie."

Thaddeus tried to look pleased, but Terry could tell it was anything but easy.

"That's great, Terry. Now if we can just convince the police you're not guilty."

"You mean you don't buy the fact that I'm guilty?"

"Of course not. The whole thing is ridiculous."

"Got any idea who really did it?" Terry said. "'Cause I'm fresh out."

"Not off hand. I mean, couldn't Joey have put the coke and money in your locker?"

"Yeah, that makes sense," Terry said. "He put it in my locker, then called his killers up and had them waste him and his brother."

"I'm sorry, "Thaddeus said. "This whole thing is confusing to me."

"You have any idea who killed Joey, Ray and Rosalie?"

"Well, it could have been anybody who was involved in the crime. It might be Nicky, but it could also be that Willie Hudson guy."

"Could be," Terry said. "But I don't think Nicky Baines feels like Willie was involved."

"What the hell do you mean?"

"I mean that Willie was just with me as a guest at Nicky's warehouse. After a long and not so pleasant talk, Nicky decided that both Willie and I are judged not-guilty of ripping him off."

Thaddeus started to rub his nose with his thumb.

"Where's the waiter around here?"

"They don't bother with waiters here. It's considered too bourgeois."

Thaddeus tried out a little laugh. It died in his throat.

"So he let you both go. I wonder why. Maybe it was just a trick. He could be following you."

He looked over Terry's shoulder as if he were expecting Alexander or one of Nicky's other guys to appear from around the corner.

"No," Terry said, in a matter of fact way. "I think it's because he's a good judge of people. He knew I didn't have it in me to kill three people. Or, for that matter, to rob his shipment of coke."

Thaddeus rubbed his chin and looked jumpy. Terry had never seen him this way before. He liked it.

"I don't know, Terry. I bet he is following you. He probably thinks you're lying. Like the cops undoubtedly do. Maybe it's time to give yourself up. The more you run, the guiltier you look. Walk in and we'll get a serious lawyer and mount a serious defense."

"Give myself up, huh? That the best you've got? I thought you believed in me. Like totally."

"I do. Of course. But I'm only saying how it looks. They have the drugs, the money…We could cop a plea. Tell them you're new to New York, how Joey conned you into stealing the dope. You wanted to be a player, so…"

"I don't think so. Thaddeus," Terry interrupted. "It sounds a little lame to me."

"Terry, listen. I'm speaking as your friend."

Terry looked at him. At his handsome face, his serious, deeply concerned eyes. The thought that he had believed him in the past, believed every word he had said, made his stomach turn.

He was sick and angry and more than anything he wanted to reach across the table and put his hands around Thaddeus' neck.

"Terry, are you all right?"

"Yeah, just fine. You were talking about friends."

Now Thaddeus' face was changing. There was something not so kind and concerned in his eyes. Something angry and scary as well. He could feel Thaddeus's heavy presence bearing down on him.

"That's right. I want to do the right thing by you, Terry."

"Of course you do," Terry said.

"I'm not sure I like your tone, Terry."

"No? What tone is that?"

"Insolent. I think that's the word."

"Insolent. I don't think so. 'Angry' might work. And 'tired.' Tired of lies."

"Whose lies?"

Terry smiled. He felt an urgent need to confront Thaddeus with what he knew, but it wasn't the right time. He wasn't wearing a wire and if he told him now, he would give his dear friend time to come up with a suitable alibi. Still, he had to let him know something. He had only two days before Nicky came to look for him again.

"Thaddeus, let's cut the shit. I know."

"You know what?"

"A lot of things. Like, for instance, who really wrote *The Debt*."

Thaddeus swallowed hard. Terry could feel the inner strain he was going through. Trying to keep his face friendly, open. Could you will your teeth to get whiter so you'd appear friendlier, honest, better? If anyone could, Thaddeus could.

"I wonder what you mean by that, Terry?"

"I mean I opened Gina's desk and I saw the manuscript. Written in her hand. And I photographed the first sixteen pages. Many of them had notes written to herself about how she had to work harder to please you."

"So that *was* you in there the other night when we came home. I heard something upstairs. But I never thought that you would…"

"Have the nerve? Doubt the master's word? I might have agreed with you a few weeks ago. But I surprised myself. It's a new ball game, Thaddeus."

Thaddeus' hands were clenched into fists. Terry's heartbeat so fast he was having trouble breathing.

"You know? And what will you do with your knowledge?"

"That's an interesting question. You played me for a mark, Thaddeus. From day one."

"Not true. I've always liked you, Terry. Think of our many discussions, playing football in the park together. I introduced you to my friends and you shone. I introduced you to the real New York. You think I would have done all that for a mere mark? No, Terry, you don't understand at all. There are things I have to explain to you. We have much to discuss, my friend."

"I'm here. Talk."

"Not here, Terry. What I have to say is complex and could greatly impact your life. I'll tell you what. I'm renting Peter Beard's windmill in Montauk while he's in Africa. I've always wanted to show it to you. The most amazing spot and Peter has all his photos on the walls. It's the kind of place a budding superstar should hang in. Come tomorrow night. Meet me there at, say, ten o'clock? We can drink, howl at the moon and really talk, Terry. Say nothing to anyone until then and I promise you that you'll be very happy that you did."

"I don't know, Thaddeus."

"Trust me. This one last time, my friend. You may not know it yet, but you've just become a very lucky guy."

Terry waited, feigned that he was mulling it over.

"Okay. You've done a lot for me, so I guess I owe you

this much. I'll be there at ten. You'll have your shot, Thaddeus."

"Good. You won't be sorry."

Thaddeus rose from his seat and smiled at Terry in his most charming manner, then turned and left the room.

Minutes after Thaddeus had gone into the night, Kathy came in from where she had been waiting on the street. She squeezed his arm and put her head on his shoulder.

"What did Thaddeus have to say to you?' she said.

"He wants me to go to meet him in Montauk tomorrow night."

"You told him you knew?"

"Yeah, and he wants to make me an offer."

"I know what his offer is going to be. A bullet in your head."

" But we have to get him on tape. It would be too easy for him to deny everything."

"So you go," Kathy said. "We'll figure out a plan to nail him. But first you've got to see someone else."

"Gina."

"Gina. If we can win her over to our side, we'll be one step closer."

They nodded at one another. Terry reached over and placed his hand on hers.

CHAPTER THIRTY

Terry met Gina Wade in the Neptune Polish restaurant just a few blocks from her home across from Tompkins Square Park. Her hair wasn't combed, which was unthinkable for her. She looked nervous, kept rubbing her thumb and forefinger together.

They ordered coffee. Terry spoke softly and tried for a reassuring tone.

"Gina, as you know, I've grown to like you."

She smiled from one side of her mouth, but her eyes registered suspicion.

"The feeling goes both ways, Terry. But I have a feeling you're not here to propose."

"No, not exactly. What I have to say...well, it's difficult to put into words."

Gina sipped her coffee and looked at him dead-on.

"Try being direct," she said. "That usually works for me."

"All right then. Gina, I know everything."

"That's admirable, Terry. But maybe you better it narrow it down for me. Are we talking about knowing everything in the entire world or just about New York City?"

She opened her purse and took out a Lucky. She snapped open her lighter and lit the cigarette with one try.

"I know that you wrote Thaddeus' novel. I know that you were, at the very least, involved in the killings of Joey and Ray and probably in the murder of Rosalie Torres."

Gina took another drag off her cigarette and attempted to look sophisticated as she blew two jets of smoke from her nostrils. But her right hand was shaking. Hmm. Very interesting. And I suppose you have evidence to back these astonishing assertions up."

She smiled and controlled the nerves in her hand.

"Not that much. Just this."

He reached into his coat pocket and took out the purple amulet he had taken from her apartment.

Gina's mouth dropped open and her eyes suddenly were filled with panic.

"Where did you get that?"

"I found it in the park, baby. Where you left it. The night you shot Joey and Ray."

Her eyes burned through him as she spoke: "That's absurd, Terry. I've never been any where u near the Glen Span Arch."

As soon as the words had slipped out of her mouth, she wished she could suck them back in again.

"Hmm," Terry said. "I wonder how you knew that the Gardello brothers were murdered under the Glen Span Arch."

This time her voice quivered ever so slightly.

"The same way you know. I read it in the *Times*."

"Sorry, Gina. It wasn't in the *Times*. I've read everything written about it. The Arch was never mentioned."

"Well, somebody told me, then."

"The cops, maybe?"

"Yes, that's right. The police."

"Funny they told you. Because I asked them all about it and they wouldn't say a word." It was a lie, but he was pretty sure he was on firm ground.

Gina looked down at her fork. For a second Terry thought she might pick it up and stab him in the face.

He smiled at her in an understanding manner and continued.

"Look, Gina, I understand how it is. You were just a kid from the sticks. You ran into a brilliant manipulator who got you to give up everything for him. He told you some stories about his life and you wanted to help him. Isn't that how it was?"

"Yes. I was just making notes about his friends and then the book seemed to be born without my even trying. I had a voice for it and the plot seemed to create itself. I had to keep going."

Terry took her hand and nodded silently.

"Of course. And you felt guilty for writing it because initially it was his idea."

"Yes. I did. It wasn't really mine. I should have stopped but it was like magic. I couldn't stop."

"Of course. Because you're an artist. As we said at lunch a while back, all art is a kind of collaboration."

"Not with Thaddeus. He said the book was always his. That I was just the vehicle through which his vision was being created."

"And you let him claim authorship because you loved him."

"Yes, and because he has been hurt so often. His father molested him when he was only six. They lived in an abandoned school bus. His mother was on speed. They both beat him. And he's a genius. You've listened to him.

No one can talk like he does. When he comes into a room, no lights are needed. You know that, Terry. You love him as much as I do."

Terry took a deep breath.

"Loved him," he said. "He set me up for murder. A murder that someone else committed. Was it you, Gina?"

"No. He wanted me to, but I couldn't. But I was there. All my life I've loved transgressive behavior. Firbank, Sadism. And that night, murder. I wanted to see Joey die. I didn't know his brother would be along."

"But who actually pulled the trigger?"

"It was those two cops, Lazenby and Green. Thaddeus promised them a new life in Hollywood. But you have to understand. They had to do it. Joey found out that I wrote the novel and he was blackmailing Thaddeus for the last three years. He demanded that we take him with us to Hollywood, that we make deal for him to make his own movies under our production deal. We couldn't have that. We couldn't stand him anymore."

She tried out a sickly smile at Terry, as though she were trying to convince herself that all this was right and justified.

"And what about Rosalie?"

"She found out. That's how Joey was. He couldn't shut up. He told her. She hadn't asked for a piece of the action yet, but you knew that was going to happen soon. Money sticks to people's minds. They can't pull it off no matter how hard they try."

She looked down at her coffee and then said in a very low voice.

"There are things you don't know, Terry. Many things. You're an amateur."

"Not anymore. Try me."

She blew out two jets of smoke and seemed to shift gears.

"When I met Thaddeus, I'd just gotten out of New Haven Mental Hospital. I'd been in for a year for manic depression. It runs in my family, Terry. The Wade family tradition of polite cocktail-hour drinks and pill-taking has ended in five suicides and several automobile crackups which might as well been called suicides."

"Was Thaddeus a patient there?"

"No, he was a volunteer. When I met him, he was in his third year and he had a double major, English Literature and Psychology. Volunteering as an aide was part of his clinical work. Terry, there was no one else like him. He was funny, charming. He quickly won over many of the patients on the ward. No one could resist him. Several of the shrinks there became jealous of him. They wanted him out. But the patients loved him. He played games with us, he really listened to our stories."

"And you fell in love with him?"

"Of course. Just as you have, Terry."

Terry blushed.

"It's all right," Gina said. "He's a magician. When he turns on the charm, when he looks into your eyes, you feel as though you're the only person in the world he cares about. I was in bad shape. I won't bore you with my family story or tell you how many times my father, Arthur, raped me. Or how many times I told my mother and her response was to smack me as hard as she could in the face."

Terry felt a wave of sympathy. He took Gina's hand as he spoke: "Here's the truth, Gina. You have to confess. Look at your story, how touching it is. You loved this guy so much you even wrote his book for him and gave him all the credit. You even covered up murder for him. You tell it to a jury and it won't be you who goes to jail for life. Or worse."

"You're very sweet, Terry," Gina said. "But you don't understand. Thaddeus and I are getting married."

She looked at him in a way that suggested she had gone over the edge into a sphere of madness that he would never be able to reach. Still, he had to try.

"Gina? That's insane."

But she was smiling, hearing voices from some dark hallway in her mind.

"No, Terry. It's beautiful. He asked me just a few days ago. He's done with running around with models and starlets. In L.A., we'll be stars. We'll have a home in Beverly Hills. And my name will go up before the titles. So I'll get the credit I lost on *The Debt*."

She gave him a triumphant little smile.

"Gina," Terry said, holding hand tighter. "You know better than any of that. It's just a fantasy. Thaddeus is marrying you so that you can never testify against him."

"No, Terry. He loves me. It's for real. I can have a Jaguar. We can travel. We are going to be royalty, Terry."

Her face lit up like a smiling doll's. There was nothing real about it anymore.

"Gina, listen. He's sold you a bill of goods. Once you're in your new dream house, how long do you think he's going to keep you around? You won't see it coming. But that won't stop it. Maybe he'll suggest a fun weekend in Palm Springs. There's a nice stretch of desert out there. A great place to bury your body."

She looked down at her coffee and then said in a very low voice, "He'd never do that, Terry. He needs me too much. He'll find the talent with his charm, but it will be me who develops the stories. We'll be a perfect team."

He wanted to slap her face, to tell her to snap out of it.

But it wouldn't have done any good. Thaddeus had worked his dark magic on her.

He thought of his power, his uncanny ability to dominate your attention. He remembered his power to make you feel that your own thoughts were small, pathetic and that you had no way to move forward without following his black flag.

Terry sat there silently, trying to figure how the scenario would play out if he could get her to tell the truth. It might convince a few people, but what would Thaddeus' lawyers do to her? They'd say she was lying, that she was the typical talentless girlfriend who wished she could have written the novel. That she copied the typed version to make it seem like she'd done it. She'd be portrayed as a neurotic, a dreamer who lived in some gauzy fantasy that she was a great artist, when all she was in reality was a slightly talented columnist.

And they'd pin the murders on her.

They'd wipe the floor with her. She couldn't bring Thaddeus down. Not alone, anyway.

He looked at her, and a tear came rolling down her cheek. Maybe she wasn't completely gone after all.

"You think I'm mad, don't you. Terry? Maybe you're right. But you know I can't go against him. Not now. He's too big, Terry. No one can bring him down."

"What if I could get a confession from him? On tape? Then we'd have what we need."

"But how could you? He would never confess."

"Maybe. But you miss one thing about him, his Achilles heel."

"I don't under—"

"His grandiosity. He not only wants to rule the world, but not very deep down, he wants the world to know how he did it."

"You're wrong, Terry. You're going to get yourself killed."

Her hands were shaking. Terry held them tightly.

"Listen, Gina, just do me and yourself a favor. For the next few days just treat Thaddeus like you always do. Don't mention I talked to you. I'll get what we need. And if you testify, I'll get you the best possible deal. You'll be rid of him. You'll be able to write under your own name. Tell the real story."

She looked shaky, blew smoke from both nostrils and slowly nodded her head in agreement.

"Okay," she said. "I'll try."

CHAPTER THIRTY-ONE

Kathy went back to her apartment at two in the morning. She knew it was unsafe, but she had her gun, triple locks and the cops really didn't have a thing on her. They might not even be looking for her. As for Nicky Baines...well, if his boys came through her door, they were going to be coming out with holes in them. Feet first.

She was still exhausted, but even after a hot bath and a Dalmane she couldn't sleep. She tossed and turned in her bed and worried about Terry. What would they do? How could they hope to get out of the traps Thaddeus had laid for them?

Would the plan she and Terry cooked up work?

She scooted over to the edge of her bed and reached over to her bedside dresser. She pulled open the only drawer, the place where she usually kept a paperback to read. But there was no longer a book there. Instead, she fingered her gun.

Her nerves were bad. Very bad. She felt as though something inside of her was trembling. Like a violin string.

Then she heard a noise. It seemed to be coming from the front room.

* * *

She slid from her bed, slipped into her jeans and a sweater and picked up the gun.

She tread lightly into her hallway, walked down it slowly, holding the gun with two hands, ready to shoot.

She slid against the wall, then peered into the front room.

There was a book lying on the floor, a novel she had been reading, one by Raymond Chandler. *The Little Sister.*

Had it just slipped off the arm of the sofa?

She moved across the room ever so slowly, went to the window, and carefully pulled back the curtains and looked outside.

Shit.

There it was again.

A green 1950s Studebaker. Refinished. Classy looking.

The same car which had been there last night.

They were watching her. But which "they?" The cops? Nicky Baines? Someone who worked for Thaddeus?

Not knowing made her crazy with fear, and the fear sickened her. She didn't want to feel afraid of them. She hated herself for feeling this way.

She wanted to race out in the street with her gun blazing and fire into the driver's seat.

Even if she couldn't see who was behind the wheel. They were just up the street, too far to get a clear look.

Which they undoubtedly knew.

She pulled the curtains together and slumped down on the couch.

Who was it? Nicky Baines? Maybe he believed she had something to do with it. Or the crooked cops, Lazenby and Greene?

She couldn't attack them. She'd end up dead on the

street. She just had to see it through.

Wait...

Keep waiting...

Though it was driving her nuts.

CHAPTER THIRTY-TWO

One night later and it was colder again. The ocean winds made the leaves flutter through Amagansett like startled birds. Terry sat in the back of The Point Bar and Grill in Montauk. He nursed a Jack Daniels on the rocks. He had told himself not to have this drink, but his nerves were frayed, his head and neck still aching from the beating Alexander had given him.

He wished Kathy was with him, but they couldn't risk being seen together by Thaddeus. She was waiting for him to drive out to her motel. He would stop briefly, honk his horn, then take off again toward the windmill. At which point she would follow behind him.

She'd pull into the woods surrounding the windmill and listen on her two-way radio.

At least he hoped she would. It was a cloudy day and he feared the signal emanating from his own radio would somehow be distorted or even altogether eliminated by the weather. Now he remembered the old windmill, all the way out to the edge of the land at Montauk Point, next to a steep cliff, with a long drop to the rocks and ocean below.

He had been out to the windmill that very afternoon. Making sure Thaddeus wasn't there. He saw the property, the drop to the rocks and beach below. He had made his half-assed plan.

He just hoped Kathy did her part.

Now it was down to the nitty-gritty. If either of them failed, he might end up dashed on those freaking rocks below the windmill, his brains sliding off into the cold sea.

He remembered the signal they'd come up with: If anything went wrong, Terry had only to say the phrase, "That's very unfortunate," and she'd come inside, her gun in her hand.

Knowing she was a much better shot than him made him feel a little better.

He took the last sip of his whiskey and got up.

No more excuses. He was going to kick some ass.

It had started to rain, and Kathy's left windshield wiper didn't work. She found herself crouching forward, trying to see through the raindrops as she headed for the windmill. Sitting on the seat next to her was her radio. Christ, what if it didn't work in the rain? That was a dumb thought. Of course it would. She'd be close enough to the house.

It was all going to work out just fine. Like she knew it would. Nothing to worry about, nothing at all.

Except for one thing. This green Studebaker which was about forty feet behind her. The same one which had been watching her at her home. Christ, they had followed her all the way from the Village. Who the hell could it be? Those two detectives Lazenby and Green, who had almost arrested Terry one block from his house?

What if they were following her? This whole meet with Thaddeus could be a setup to catch Terry.

Or even kill Terry.

"We told him to halt, but he kept running. He turned and aimed at us and we were forced to fire."

She looked in her rearview mirror as she made a turn and for a second the Studebaker wasn't there. But she had no sooner breathed a sigh of relief than it came into sight again.

Whoever it was must have slowed down. Was it because of the increasing volume of the rain? Or was it because the two cops didn't want to scare her off?

She felt her stomach churn. And she began to silently pray.

She took a left turn off down the sandy road which led to the windmill. It was maybe fifty yards ahead. She had to turn off on the fire road. There it was just ahead of her. She turned to the left and drove into a little structure made of tree branches that Terry had made this afternoon.

She looked back down the fire road. No green Studebaker. Thank God. At least for now she'd lost them.

She got out of the car, protected from the rain by the leaves all around her. Her radio in one hand and her purse with her gun in the other, she shut the door.

And turned on the radio to listen.

Terry walked up the driveway, feeling the gun in a shoulder holster inside his jacket like an absurd weight. Was it totally obvious he was armed?

Jesus, of course it was. He stopped, took off the shoulder holster and threw it in the leaves. Then he stuck the gun in the back of his pants.

He had an absurd vision of himself reaching for the gun and pulling the trigger, thus shooting his own ass off.

He pulled his jacket down and hoped he had hidden the handgun.

He climbed to the front door of the darkened windmill. Stared to rap on it, but then noticed it was open a crack.

He pushed it the rest of the way and walked inside.

There seemed to be no one there at all.

He looked around the room. A ten-speed bike lying on its side, a pile of magazines on the bamboo coffee table.

He could hear the sound of the ocean crashing against the rocks fifty feet below.

Then he heard what he thought were footsteps from up-stairs.

"Thaddeus?" he called.

No answer.

He called again as he started up the spiral wooden staircase to the top floor. Again, there was nothing.

He reached the top, half expecting Thaddeus to jump him.

Instead, Thaddeus stood with his back to him, by the open window on the ocean side. He stared out at the rain and the cloud-hidden moon.

"Isn't it beautiful, Terry?" Thaddeus said.

"Yeah, gorgeous," Terry said.

Thaddeus indicated a cane back chair and Terry cautiously sat down.

"I was just thinking about you and your novel. Making any progress?"

"Not lately," Terry said. "I've been busy running from the cops."

"Of course, you have," Thaddeus said. "That's very time consuming. What was your novel called anyway?"

"I can't believe you don't remember the title," Terry

said. "After all, you thought of it."

"Yes, I've always been good with titles. *Bad Boy*, wasn't it? The adventures of a bad boy journalist in New York, plowing his way through all the single women in town, snorting coke, drinking himself insensate and then, finally, seeing the light with a nice girl. A girl like the charming Kathy."

"Yes, that was the idea," Terry said.

"Well, you seem to be moving at turtle speed. But I understand. Novels are exhausting to work on. They take years sometimes."

Terry nodded his head but said nothing. Where the hell was Thaddeus going with all this?

"You see, Terry, of course you can write that novel. But why haven't you? If you're anything like me, you probably haven't written it because you feel ambivalent about the entire enterprise."

"Like you?" Terry said. "You have a best seller and a movie of your novel opening in a few days. Even if you didn't really write it."

Terry expected Thaddeus to be unnerved by that comment, but his old mentor was ready.

"So you said the other night. Listen, my friend. What proof do you have?"

"Like I told you, I saw the handwritten manuscript in Gina's desk. I have pictures of Gina's notes to herself."

"Did it ever occur to you that Gina handwrote the novel to try and capture my rhythms, my use of metaphor? Much like Hemingway copied all of Sherwood Anderson's *Winesburg, Ohio*. She thought it would help her, a blocked novelist, break through. I knew all about it and encouraged her."

"And I suppose she wrote editorial ideas to herself as well. Sorry, Thaddeus. It doesn't wash."

Thaddeus sighed and lit a cigarette.

"You're wrong. I worked on that novel for years and years. Gina is a wonderful person but mentally unstable. You really don't think anyone will believe a mere columnist wrote that book. But let's change the subject for a minute. You just said that I have a best seller and in a technical way that's true. But the truth is, it didn't really sell all that many books. Nothing comparted to the stars of the romance genre or the sci-fi fantasy world. So what am I supposed to do now? Sit down for another ten years and write another book? And what if it tanks? Then I'm a middle-aged man with one-book syndrome and nowhere to go. Like so many other writers. No, Terry, that's not my fate and it shouldn't be yours either."

Terry felt a little shaky. He'd thought that he had the major bit of evidence against Thaddeus, but his dear friend had just shrugged it off like it was nothing at all.

"So what's your plan?" Terry said, trying to recoup.

"In a word, Hollywood. When you have a hit book, that's the time to strike. Forget book number two and make a deal for a production company. And as luck would have it, I've already made such a deal. Millions of dollars for the first three pictures, an office on the lot at Fox. A TV deal as well. And, of course, I need writers. Great writers with great stories. Writers like you, Terry."

"Is that right? How thoughtful of you."

Thaddeus laughed and smiled at Terry with his old warmth and charm.

"You're doubtful. Fine, then let me explain. Twentieth believes that the really great writers of today are journalists.

They're the ones who have the ideas. They've done the stories. Why did you quit teaching? To see the real world. And write about it. And you have, brilliantly. But what do you get? A couple thousand bucks from a magazine and then on to the next one. You can never stop to get a breath. At this rate, how long will it be until you flame out? Hollywood is your next best move and we'll go together."

Now it was Terry's turn to laugh.

"Gee, Thaddeus, aren't you forgetting you framed me for killing three people?"

"I acted hastily, foolishly. Regrettable, and I am truly sorry. But the good news is I can undo it as easily as I set it up. There's a crazy vet I know who hung around Joey. A guy named Willie Hudson. He always wanted to be in the movies. I have a witness ready to say that they saw him do the whole thing, including killing Ray and the unfortunate Rosalie."

"You're kidding? Willie? I know him. He had nothing to do with any of this. For Chrissakes, Thaddeus."

Thaddeus walked around the room and shook his head, as though he was a teacher slightly miffed by his star pupil's inability to grasp the central concept of the discussion.

"Terry, Terry, Terry. You have to grasp the big picture. Don't be a loser. Willie Hudson is the perfect fall guy. A drifter, an angry..."

"Nigger? Go ahead and say it, Thaddeus. The perfect fall guy, indeed."

"I wasn't going to say the 'N' word," Thaddeus said. "But since you brought it up, it doesn't hurt us that he's black. People are sick of black rage. The Panthers were our idols and look how they turned out. Really just aging thugs. Face it, Terry. Black people have been given every break and look at them. It's tragic, of course."

"Oh yeah. I can tell you're broken up by it all. You kill three people and you walk away and let someone else, a really decent man, by the way, take the rap?"

Thaddeus got up from his chair and walked to the window. The rain blew in on him. He wiped it off his face and smiled.

"You don't understand, Terry. Let me try one more time. Greatness in any field, politics business, sports or films, requires sacrifice. Think of it this way: there are emperors who are remembered by the pyramids and there are the stone carriers who slaved to build them. Which will you be, Terry?"

"You really believe that? That's how you see life?"

"Of course. All great men believe it. Once the pyramid is built do you really think anyone cares about the names of the thousands of slaves who piled on the stones? No. Still, they gave their lives for a noble cause. Just as Joey, Ray and Rosalie did. And soon Willie too. And we, the emperors, owe them the greatest pictures we can make. Not just moneymakers, but classics. That way their hapless lives will mean something in the end."

Terry felt his stomach churn.

"You do mean it, don't you? This is really you, the real Thaddeus Bryant."

"Yes, I live by this code, Terry, and you should too. Trust me, whatever your little Bible school morality tells you, you really don't want to end up as a stone carrier."

The transmission on Kathy's radio was breaking up now. She moved her antennae around a little and the signal became sharper again. She reached into her purse and felt for her gun. The grip felt good in her hand. She opened her car door and dropped her purse in the front seat. And moved away from the shelter, through the beating rain, toward the windmill.

Terry tried to remember what Thaddeus had just said. Had he really admitted killing Joey, Ray and Rosalie? In so many words, yes, but not exactly. He needed him to say it, so he couldn't wiggle out of it. But now Thaddeus was talking again.

"You know what I want our first project to be, Terry?"

"What?"

"*Bad Boy.*"

"My novel? But I haven't even written it yet."

"Right, and maybe you never will. But you will write it as a screenplay. Think of it, a screenplay about a would-be writer who gets lost in wild seventies New York, snorting coke, running around with models. It's the real world you've already lived, so you could write the hell out of it."

"Yeah, sounds great," Terry said. "There's only one problem. I don't know anything about writing screenplays."

"What difference does that make? You'll learn. How hard can it be? And if you struggle a bit, we'll get someone to help you."

"Like Gina helped you?"

"You keep bringing that up, Terry. Forget it. That ship has sailed."

"No. I don't think so Thaddeus. It's still tied up at the dock. And I still have very sharp photos of it."

Thaddeus shook his head and sighed heavily.

"Gina is so vain. I told her to get rid of that thing."

Now Terry got up and walked toward Thaddeus.

"But she held onto it. Just in case the man she worshipped tried to make her have an accident in Disneyland. And Joey must have found out too. How'd he manage to do that?"

Thaddeus sipped his whiskey and sighed.

"Why not tell you? That was also Gina's fault. She came up to my place one night when Joey was there. In my spare bedroom, sleeping off a night of debauchery. She was a little loaded herself and started an argument with me about the way "her novel" was going to go. Unfortunately, Joey had done some coke and was still wide awake. He heard the whole thing. Soon after, he put the finger on me for hush money. In the end he had to be sacrificed. But forget all of that. We're moving beyond all that. You'll get off and we'll head out to Hollywood. Partners. Emperors."

"You still haven't answered me. What if Gina makes a deal with the cops?"

"That will never happen. I haven't told you the happy news yet. We're going to be married. She'll come with us."

"Really. But if she doesn't, if she's scared to go with her murderer husband. Look at it this way. Some of the sharks in Hollywood might not care if you are accused of murder. But they will definitely want to know who they are giving millions of dollars to. The brilliant author of *The Debt*, who in reality never wrote a single word? Oh no, they'll care about that, big time. You know, they might even give *her* a deal instead of you. That would be just perfect."

Thaddeus took a step toward him. Terry reached behind his back. Slowly.

"I don't think so," Thaddeus said. "I don't think they'll

give Gina anything at all."

He smiled and pointed to a canvas drop cloth which lay over something in the corner.

Terry tried to keep his hard-won cool, but this was something he simply wasn't ready for.

"Go ahead, partner. Look."

Terry knew he shouldn't take his eyes off of Thaddeus for even a second, but he couldn't resist. The drop cloth seemed to have a life of its own. It was as though it was beckoning him to come look and see what lay beneath it.

He walked over to the corner, keeping one eye on Thaddeus.

He reached down and pulled the cloth back.

It was Gina all right, but not the pert, New York sophisticate he knew so well. This was a white-faced Gina with her tongue hanging out of her mouth, and her eyes popped open in horror.

"You killed her. Strangled her. That is...most unfortunate."

"That's right, Terry. I did. I'm quite strong, you know."

Kathy heard the code words, "that's most unfortunate" and started for the windmill. She slid in the mud but kept going and was only fifteen yards away when she saw Detective Lazenby running toward her through the woods. He was about fifty yards behind and to the west of her. But his sight line was obscured by trees.

"Halt, you're under arrest!"

Kathy figured things quickly. If she went on into the windmill, she would lead him right in with her. Terry would be shot and killed by the son of a bitch.

No, she had to lead him away.

She turned and shot over Lazenby's head.

He pulled his gun and tried to fire back but he couldn't get a clear shot.

Kathy dodged back into the greenery and kept going, back the way she'd come, toward her car.

Lazenby slipped in the mud but got up quickly and followed behind her, shouting for her to "halt" twice more.

Back inside the windmill, Terry was badly shaken by Gina's corpse.

"I told her not to go see you. I told her..."

"Of course you did," Thaddeus said. "But she never could keep her mouth shut. I was going to wait until we got out there to do it. Maybe drown her out in Malibu. But it's better this way. I'll take that wire you're wearing on your chest now, Terry."

"Fuck you, Thaddeus," he said. Terry tried to reach for his gun, but Thaddeus had already leapt at him and had his hands around Terry's throat.

Still bent over Gina's body as he was, Terry tried to duck down and shake Thaddeus off. He got one hand loose, then turned and kneed Thaddeus in the groin.

Thaddeus screamed and fell backwards, losing purchase on Terry's throat. Terry stood up and punched him in the face. Thaddeus fell backwards toward the open window.

The waves crashed below them as they struggled.

Terry tried to reach for his gun again, but Thaddeus ripped at his hands and the gun fell out on the windmill floor.

They battled and clawed and Terry looked down and

saw that Thaddeus had ripped the tape recorder from his chest.

Terry punched him again and Thaddeus fell back against the wall but found an oar which was lying next to the window. He picked it up and slammed it against Terry's temple.

Terry was dizzy, off balance. He tried to reach for Thaddeus' shirt, but Thaddeus hit him with the oar again. Terry fought back, knocking the oar out of Thaddeus' hands. Thaddeus reached down to pick it up, but Terry kicked him in the face.

Thaddeus fell backwards, almost unconscious. Terry stood over him, still dizzy.

Had he won the fight?

He turned to look at Gina again. He couldn't quite believe she was dead. But one glance at her bluish pallor convinced him.

When he turned back to deal with Thaddeus, he was stunned to see him reaching for the gun, which was almost in his grasp.

The branches whipped Kathy's face as she headed back to her car. She was only a few feet away and had seemingly lost Lazenby in the woods.

She'd get in, and head down the fire road. Christ, she might just make it.

"Going somewhere?"

She turned and saw a drenched and mud splattered Detective Green coming out from a grove of trees.

In his hand was his automatic.

"I found your car a few minutes ago, kid. I knew you'd

have to come back here. Drop your gun."

Kathy knew she had no chance. She dropped it in the leaves and mud.

"What a genius you are," Kathy said. "So, Thaddeus has the two of you."

"Hey, all we did was run security for Joey. Now come along and be a good girl. I don't want to hurt you anymore than necessary. I'm actually a very nice guy, which the people in Hollywood are going to find out. Lazenby and I are starting out as consultants, but soon we'll be doing our own cop films. Man, Thaddeus is going to set us up, sweetheart. Might even do some acting too. When actors play cops it's just so fucking lame, you know?"

"Yeah, especially that part about honoring the badge and doing the right thing."

"What would you know about it? We did all that for years and all we got for it was a trashing by a bunch of liberals. Now we aim to get some of our own. It's kind of a shame that you won't be around to check out our films. 'Cause this is your last day on earth."

He aimed the gun at her. Kathy winced, put up her arms in a defensive position. Any second the bullets would tear through her flesh and she'd fall next to her car. She waited, terrified, and then heard a loud crunching sound.

She peeked through her fingers and saw Detective Green slump to the ground. Blood oozed from the back of his head, which Willie Hudson had staved in with a thick tree branch.

"Willie! What the hell?"

She started laughing in a near hysterical way as she ran to him and threw her arms around him.

"How did you…"

He laughed and held her, then shrugged.

"I told Terry I wouldn't help him. Then I went to bed that night and I had these thoughts that wouldn't go away. Thought of Terry getting me out of trouble with Nicky and then I had like a vision of Terry lying in a woods somewhere with his throat slit. Man, I come down to see you a few nights ago. To find out where the crazy bastard is. Then I figured I just better watch over you instead. I knew he'd get in touch with you soon."

"That was you in the Studebaker?" Kathy said.

"Yeah, had that car for a long time. Still runs good though."

"Willie, you followed me all the way out here?"

"That's right. Hope you don't mind."

"Mind?"

She kissed him on the cheek.

"You're the best, Willie. But, listen, we have to get out of here now. The other cop is coming soon."

Willie gave a small smile.

"No he ain't. I used some of my old SEAL training on his ass. Got 'em both with this one branch. He fell pretty good, and when he tried to get up I hit him again, jest like Green here, right in the back of his skull."

Kathy couldn't help but laugh.

"Willie Hudson," she said. "You're a goddamned hero."

"Yeah but be all for nothing if we don't save Terry Brennan. Come on, Kathy, see if you can't run in this goop."

Thaddeus had nearly reached the gun. Terry thought about diving across the room on top of him. But Thaddeus was too far away, about sixty-five feet away, it seemed. Then Terry realized he was far too dizzy to dive anywhere. The room looked like he was seeing it through the wrong end of a telescope. Thaddeus was so small, but even so, Terry could see his feral smile.

Terry stumbled backwards.

Thaddeus had the gun now. He was in a sitting position and pointing the barrel at Terry's chest.

Terry looked around. He was nowhere near the front steps.

Only the open window was close enough for escape.

But escape to where?

He heard Thaddeus laugh.

"Go ahead, Terry. There's your way out. It's only a hundred feet down to the ocean. You might survive."

Thaddeus laughed and with his free hand picked up the tape recorder from the floor.

"You had a real shot, Terry. Man, you and I could have had it all. Now jump, you son of a bitch."

Terry found himself moving toward the window, almost as though he was unconscious.

Then he stepped off into the night.

Thaddeus tried to get up, but Terry's kick had made him woozy. He took a couple of deep breaths, tried to rise again but found blood streaming down his face.

He stopped, wiped his face with his handkerchief.

The son of a bitch was tougher than he thought.

But, in the end, it had gone down as he knew it would.

He found a chair, leaned on it, and slowly got to his feet.

Then he heard the sound of people crashing through the

underbrush.

A woman's voice.

"Oh Christ, Willie, look!"

Willie and Kathy had approached the windmill from the west side. They had walked along a narrow trail which ran alongside a steep cliff.

As they came out of the trees, they stood transfixed. There, thirty feet in front of them Terry Brennan hung from the slats of one of the windmill arms. His body dangled over the rocks, beach and ocean below.

There was a small amount of grass between him and the cliff side.

"He's trying to pull the windmill arm down closer to the land." Kathy said.

"Yeah but look."

Kathy saw what Willie meant. Though Terry was a trim, fit person his weight was still too much for the windmill arm slats.

They watched in horror as one of the slats ripped out of the arm. It looked as though he would fall then, but somehow Terry grabbed the next slat, and pulled the arm closer.

"Hang on, Terry," Willie cried and ran towards his friend. Kathy was right behind him.

On the windmill Terry felt his fingers splitting. He couldn't hang on much longer. And who was that yelling at him?

From inside the windmill Thaddeus saw the two of them, guns in hand, running toward the back of the windmill.

He expected them to look over the side and see the broken body of their hero being tossed by the waves.

But instead they were looking up...

Christ, was it possible that the son of a bitch was hanging up there by the slats?

He quickly thought of his options and realized that as long as he could get away, he still had the right story.

Poor, kindhearted Gina had met with Terry, probably to get him to turn himself in. She only wanted the best for everybody. But he had strangled her and gotten away again.

The three of them might have another story but he still had the two cops on his side.

And where the hell were those worthless crooks?

God, it was so hard to find good help.

He grabbed his gun and a coat, quickly ran out the front door, and headed for his car.

Outside in the night the waves rolled into the shore, large, powerful waves which crashed against the rocks and sand.

A man might survive these waves if he was conscious and a good swimmer.

And if he was lucky as hell, he might possibly hit the beach in one piece.

But if he had just fallen from a hundred-foot drop and was knocked unconscious there was no way he'd survive.

And who was that screaming at him? Was it Kathy? Yes. But whose was the other voice?

His weight pulled the paddles towards the ground, much quicker than he had imagined when he had cased the windmill that afternoon.

And as he headed downward, he heard the slat start to

rip out of the arm.

If it came out too soon, he would still fall too far and crash into the beach which still lay a long way beneath him.

His body would break apart like a wrecked kayak.

So he held on for dear life, praying that he could get close enough to the ground to let himself have a chance of survival.

But the slat was coming loose now, and he was too far gone to grab another one.

It was over for him. He was sure of it.

Then he fell, hurtling toward the deadly rocks below.

Only he never got to the rocks.

Someone was scooping him out of the sky. And he was suddenly in the waiting arms of Willie Hudson, who grabbed him and pulled him by his shoulders just as he was going to slide by the edge of the cliff.

They both fell backwards, on to the cool wet grass.

And now Kathy Anderson was kissing him on his face and saying: "Baby...baby. Did you think you could fly?"

And beyond her he saw standing over him, rubbing his own sprained shoulder, the great, smiling face of Willie Hudson.

"Damn," he said. "Terry, next time you feel like telling me you need help, just shut the hell up. okay?"

CHAPTER THIRTY-THREE

The great spotlight lit up the sky over the Ziegfeld Theater for the grand opening of *The Debt*. The film had already gotten good word of mouth inside the industry. No, it wasn't *Casablanca*, but *The Debt* was a big, serious movie that could more than hold its own with some of the best pictures of the past decade. And New Yorkers had a special reason to root for the film. Directed by Sidney Lumet, produced by Elliot Kastner, written by Thaddeus Bryant, and starring Dustin Hoffman, George C. Scott, Genevieve Bujold, and Roy Scheider, *The Debt* was a movie which had been born in, nurtured, and come to full maturity at Elaine's.

It was a New York film all the way. In the cultural war between Hollywood and New York it would be a victory for the Big Apple.

And unlike in Hollywood, people in New York didn't forget that there was a best-selling novel which started the whole deal.

Thus, Thaddeus found him outside the theatre giving interviews to friends of his from Elaine's, reporters from *The New York Post*, the *New York Times*, and the four-year-old baby monster of gossip rags, *People* magazine.

* * *

Thaddeus finally strolled into the Ziegfeld, walking next to Mayor Ed Koch who smiled and congratulated him. It was a grand and serious opening night. A night of frayed nerves and high hopes that the world would love *The Debt*.

Everyone who mattered was there, except the true author of the book, Gina Wade. A brilliant novelist who would never write again.

Thaddeus gave her a very small thought as the picture began. So sad she felt compelled to threaten him. She should have known better than to side with that sentimental mark, Terry Brennan. For a moment he felt a pang of sadness. But then the film started and he forgot that either Gina or Terry ever existed.

There was a movie playing. HIS movie. From HIS novel. A masterpiece.

To hell with the losers.

He gave a small prayer that the world would love his creation.

And they did.

The Debt received a thunderous standing ovation. The producer, Elliot Kastner, was called to the stage, as were Sidney Lumet and the stars—Dustin Hoffman hugging Sidney and Scheider hugging Genevieve Bujold. George C. Scott, who stole the picture, got the biggest hand of all. Then Lumet stepped out and said, "And let us not forget the author of the book that *The Debt* is based on...Thaddeus Bryant."

Thaddeus started to the stage, and just for a second

wondered where the screenwriter was. He had conferred with Tod Hartley, an A-list screenwriter, for several weeks while Tod slaved over the twentieth draft of the script, but somehow he seemed to have been totally forgotten.

He reminded himself that when he got to Hollywood he would produce, not write. Writers were shit. Look what happened to Gina.

He stepped up to the stage and waved to the star-studded audience. They roared their approval.

This was it, Thaddeus thought, the greatest night of his life.

And there was so much more to come. The gala after-party at Elaine's. As he hugged the diminutive Hoffman, he could hardly wait to jump in the limo and head to the Upper East Side.

CHAPTER THIRTY-FOUR

Clarence had been in a state of near constant excitement from the day that he'd learned that *The Debt* was opening in only two days. He'd gone out and gotten himself a used tuxedo. Yes, it was a little threadbare but, amazingly, it fit him pretty well. Of course, it was a bit short in the legs and the cummerbund didn't really fit well. But who needed a cummerbund anyway? He'd just button it up and his girth would take care of the pants.

He could not wait to see all the stars. Dustin and Roy Scheider and the gorgeous Genevieve Bujold, what a living doll.

But of all of them he most wanted to see the writer of the novel, Thaddeus Bryant. Because Thaddeus had started waving to him as he left Elaine's. One of the only celebs who actually paid him any attention. And because *The Debt* was the greatest novel he had ever read (with the possible exception of *Love Story*) and also because Thaddeus was being stalked by that killer journalist, Terry Brennan.

After Thaddeus had taken the kid under his wing, introduced him to everyone in New York, practically made him a star!

And look what the creep does.

He kills three people. One of them Thaddeus' best friend.

And Terry Brennan was still on the loose.

Jesus, the guy was almost another Manson.

And he was sure, well, almost sure that the evil killer Terry Brennan was going to make an appearance at Elaine's, and that he was going to try and harm his former mentor.

But he wouldn't succeed. On no...he wouldn't get anywhere at all.

Because Clarence had his gun, old .38, oiled and ready for action.

This was a great night for New York, a great night for Thaddeus Bryant, and it might well be a great night for Clarence.

This was the night he might well become a true hero.

He would save his idol, the world's greatest writer, Thaddeus Bryant, and he would become, as a result of his bravery, a household name.

(If he showed up. He probably wouldn't show up. Why the fuck was he bringing his gun anyway? Was he stupid? Christ, he might be stupid. No, don't think that. He had a premonition. Stupid people didn't have premonitions. Or did they?)

He clipped on his tuxedo bow tie and looked down at his well-polished shoes, then stepped out of the door and headed for his destiny in New York City.

CHAPTER THIRTY-FIVE

The crowd at Elaine's was only about half as big as the mob at the Ziegfeld but much more elite. The usual stars were there, Mick Jagger, Norman Mailer, Terry Southern, Julie Christie, Jackie Bisset, the Kissingers, powerful ICM agent Esther Newberg, Woody Allen, Mariel Hemingway, Walter Cronkite, Jim Walker of Stone, Howard Freeman in his new fedora, and assorted Hamptons billionaires with their starlet girlfriends.

When the limos arrived with Lumet and the stars of the show, the entire crowd jumped up and gave them a standing ovation. Madness, adulation.

The Big Time. All Thaddeus wanted. And now was his.

Tonight there was no Bridge and Tunnel crowd at the front bar. No, tonight was a New York crème de la crème ultimate celeb night. People who had risen to the very pinnacle of New York Fame and Glory.

No room for the losers, the hangers-on.

Which didn't mean they weren't there.

Oh yes, they were still there. Just not inside. Close to seventy-five of the regular Bridge and Tunnel people were milling around outside, including Clarence.

He had made good time into the city, parked his heap around the corner and had made sure his gun was strapped on his thigh, the way he'd seen it in an old episode of *The Rockford Files*. His hair was greased back; he thought it gave him kind of a retro look. Kind of like Valentino.

He knew some of the other B and T'ers were laughing at him, but he didn't care. He was having a ball and had used his weight and girth to move into the fan front lines.

All around him flashbulbs popped as the stars were ushered into Elaine's. Clarence marveled at them all but secretly waited for his favorite to make an appearance.

The limos were lined up out front and almost all the stars were inside.

The cold champagne, the smiles of the gorgeous women.

And there, just over there, was Thaddeus Bryant stepping out of his limo with Valerie Stevenson. The actress.

Clarence wanted to scream or reach out and touch Thaddeus, but that would be so uncool. So he just smiled and looked at his idol. And at his amazing-looking girlfriend in her off-shoulder, lime green gown.

As the two beautiful people passed by Clarence, Thaddeus felt someone on his left, pressing in on him. Christ, he wished he had Lazenby and Green here to watch over him. But, unfortunately, they were in a Long Island Hospital with cracked skulls. Nervously, he turned, and with relief, recognized the big guy. Just that chunky B and T'er from the front bar, and now he smiled and said: "Hey, man." Clarence tried to reply but words wouldn't come, so he just nodded with his mouth hanging open.

"Oh my God, he spoke to me!" Clarence swallowed but his throat was dry from excitement.

As he inched forward in the line, Thaddeus thought of

his old friend, Terry Brennan. To think he had given up a goddess like Valerie for a lowly barmaid. A deep character flaw. Rooting for some bullshit version of Innocent True Love over becoming a Power Couple.

Very earnest and so very lame.

In his own way he had tried to wake Terry up. But all of that was history. And Terry was probably fish bait, floating in the mighty Atlantic. Unless, somehow…

No way. He was dead. Had to be. And so be it. A stone carrier to the end.

CHAPTER THIRTY-SIX

Inside, as the party went on with toasts and promises to work together on future projects and hugs and air kisses and blissful feelings of being at the tip top of the world, another little group huddled outside.

This group of three people was even farther away from the happy celebration than the Bridge and Tunnel mob. Two of them stood around another one who sat in a wheelchair, a slouch hat pulled low on his face.

The two standing friends had severe doubts about Terry's plan. But it was the only plan they could come up with, and the longer they stayed fugitives the worse their chances were.

It was, indeed, now or never.

Or as a slightly crazed Terry had put it: "We're all going to Elaine's. We're all attending the after-party. I wouldn't miss it for the world."

And now Nurse Kathy was pushing Terry across Second Avenue, as hospital attendant Willie helped her lift the poor invalid's wheelchair up over the curb. Willie was leading the way though the Bridge and Tunnel people, almost walking into dapper Clarence Eberhard, who gasped as he looked down at the guy in the chair.

Even though Clarence could see very little of his eyes, what he could see made him back off a little. Whoever this guy was, he meant business.

Was it possibly...could it even remotely be...Terry Brennan?

He wasn't sure. He felt paralyzed by indecision. But reached down to his leg and fondled his holster.

The two outsiders rolled their leader through the restaurant doors, by the bar, and up to Gianni, who stood at the first table welcoming in the latest celebs.

Gianni turned and stared at Willie Hudson, and Nurse Kathy Anderson.

"I'm sorry," he said. "Tonight is by invitation only. The restaurant is being rented by Twentieth Century Fox Studios for a private movie party. You may all come tomorrow and have drinks at the bar."

Kathy and Willie stepped out of the way, so that Terry could fix his laser-like eyes on Gianni.

"Gianni. Nice to see you," Terry said.

Gianni squinted his eyes, stooped down and put his face very close to Terry's.

"What the hell? Is that you, Terry?"

"You bet," Terry said. "I'll be sitting at my usual table with Thaddeus Bryant. These are my nurse and caretaker. They'll need seats as well."

"But, Terry," Gianni said.

Terry reached inside his coat, gripped his gun.

"We need our seats, Gianni. Understand?"

Gianni was not used to being spoken to in this fashion.

Ordinarily he would call a few of the other employees in the back and they would "escort" any troublemakers out of the restaurant. But there was something in Terry's eyes, something in his voice, something in the hand reaching for what could only be a loaded revolver which made the charming maître 'd acquiesce at once.

He nodded and walked ahead of Terry, Willie, and Kathy to the third table.

There sat Thaddeus Bryant and Valerie Stevenson, talking to Mick and Bianca Jagger.

Thaddeus was holding forth to Beard when he sensed something behind him.

He turned and looked at guy in the wheelchair, who was staring him down.

"Congratulations, Thaddeus. What a pleasure to see you."

Thaddeus Bryant, never at a loss for words, tried to speak. But not one word issued from his mouth. Finally, he managed a single two-syllable word, which he turned into four.

"Te...Te...Terry? How did you...?"

"Yes, spot on, Thaddeus. Nailed it on the first try."

Thaddeus looked up at the three other people who stared down at him. He swallowed deeply and managed to stand.

"What the fuck?" he said. "You and these...people... You're not invited."

He gave a kind a dismissive laugh. The laugh which usually shut Terry down. But not tonight.

"How about Gina Wade?" Terry said loudly. "Is she invited?"

A couple of the celebs at the next table overheard. Jim

Walker suddenly looked amused.

"Yeah, Thaddeus, how come Gina's not here?"

A few more people picked up on the question.

"That's right," director Arthur Penn said. "Where is my favorite columnist?"

"She wouldn't miss this," Pete Hamill said.

"You're right," Terry said, climbing out of his wheelchair. "She wouldn't miss this at all. Because this is really HER opening night. Gina Wade is the person who really wrote *The Debt*. She was a supremely talented and supremely fucked-up person who this poseur got under his thumb and gas-lighted into thinking she had to let him take all her credit. For which he was going to marry her and offer her safety and a place in society."

Now the entire festive throng grew silent. There was a rumble of anger in the audience but also a rumble of disbelief.

"That's absurd," Thaddeus screamed. "This hopeless hanger-on is wanted by the police."

He turned from Terry and addressed the now riveted crowd.

"Most of you already know the story. Terry Brennan was a nobody. He did a piece on me and took advantage of both mine and Gina's good will. And when we tired of his act and refused to see him anymore, he stalked us and now he's made up this ridiculous story."

"Yeah," Pete Hamill, the star journalist said, walking toward Terry. "Where is your proof, Terry?"

"Thought you'd never ask," Terry said. "Here are some photos of the real manuscript for *The Debt* written in Gina's hand."

"I can explain that," Thaddeus said. "She copied it to

try and get my rhythms."

"The whole book?" said Kathy.

"You? You fucking barmaid. What the fuck do you know?"

"Girl knows plenty," Willie said. "Fact is, we all know plenty about you, Thad."

"You see who he hangs out with now?" Thaddeus screamed. "Losers, street people!"

There was another gaping silence.

"Nice try, Thaddeus," Terry said. "But this little band of outsiders has your ass nailed. It's all right here on tape."

He reached into his coat and pulled out a cassette tape.

"Every word of his confession to me. He admits that he killed Joey and Ray and Rosalie Torres. And Gina Wade. With his own two hands. Because he has a producing deal with millions of dollars at Fox which would have been dead if they knew the truth. That it was Gina Wade who really wrote *The Debt*."

There was a roar from the partygoers. A roar of fury, and Thaddeus, for the first time, looked panicked.

"You couldn't have that tape, Brennan. I made you take it off before you jumped out of the window at Montauk. I destroyed it."

"Yeah," Terry said. "You did pull a mic off of me, Thaddeus. The one on my chest. But I wore a second mic on my back. You kind of forgot that one."

Thaddeus turned and looked around at the famous faces who only minutes ago were his best friends. Now they got up from their seats and closed in on him like a jury who has just found him guilty.

He looked at Terry and screamed again.

"You son of a bitch. I offered you everything. Everything!

Now you'll have nothing. Not even your life!"

Thaddeus pulled out his switchblade and dove at Terry, going for his throat. But Kathy was too quick for him. She pushed him out of the way and the knife swung wildly, missing its mark.

Suddenly, the crowd was screaming, lurching toward Thaddeus.

He pushed Kathy aside. Willie attempted to tackle him, but Terry's wheelchair was in the way. Thaddeus ran through the few people at the first table and headed for the door.

Thaddeus pushed open the doors and saw the Bridge and Tunnel people standing there in shock. He swiped at them with his knife and they leapt back.

All but one.

Clarence Eberhard stood in his path. He had missed the dialogue between the two men. All he knew was Thaddeus Bryant, his hero, had swiped at that fugitive, the low-down journalist, Terry Brennan, who had obviously come to this party to harm him. (Just as he had foreseen. He was not stupid after all!)

In fury, he reached down to his leg holster, unsnapped it and looked at the crazed journalist now running from Elaine's to hurt the great author.

"Halt," Clarence said to Terry and the two people who seemed to be with him. He pointed his Ruger in their general direction and was ready to fire.

Thaddeus Bryant stared at the big man and came to the wrong conclusion.

"Fuck you, fat man. Stand back. I'll cut you."

He stabbed at the air and the knife cut Clarence's cheek. The blood gushed down his threadbare rented tuxedo.

Clarence reached up and felt the hot blood. Suddenly, he felt like weeping. He had only wanted to help his favorite author and now his hero had stabbed him. He looked at Thaddeus, confused, and deeply wounded. For a second, he felt paralyzed. What should he do?

Who was the villain here?

Thaddeus, too, had stopped in his tracks. He now recognized Clarence as a fan of his. God, he had made a terrible mistake. The fat goof was trying to defend him from Brennan, Willie and Kathy Anderson. And he had sliced open his cheek!

He had to right this situation at once.

"Sorry, man. I thought you were with them. They're trying to kill me. Shoot them. All of them!"

Clarence was so glad that his idol had recognized and apologized to him that he turned his gun towards Terry, Willie and Kathy. (And half of the other party members who had streamed out of the restaurant.)

"I know who you are," Clarence said. "An ingrate. A jealous ingrate who hates the man who tried to help you."

He aimed the gun at Terry, who had nowhere to go.

But Clarence hesitated. It was one thing to shoot a guy attacking you, but a man who had done nothing at all to you. Was it possible that he had it wrong again?

He began to sweat and pant, his blood pressure probably going through the roof.

All he'd want to do was help the good guy.

But who was the good guy?

And to add to his discomfort, he suddenly saw himself as others did.

A three-hundred-pound fool in a used and bloody tux.

As he tried to reason all of this out, Kathy came around to his left, unseen, and gave his right arm a single karate chop. The pistol fell to the ground.

Terry was so stunned by this move that he wasted a second before he tried to bend over and pick up the gun.

Thaddeus was quicker. He knelt down and swooped the gun into his right hand. Then he laughed at Terry.

"Too slow and too dumb. Terry."

Then he shot Terry Brennan in the stomach.

Terry watched the blood come through his bandages. Red on white. Beautiful in a way.

He fell to the ground then, as an intense heat and pain shot through him.

Thaddeus Bryant turned to run away, only to be shot in the stomach by Willie Hudson.

"I heard what you had planned for me, Thaddeus. So fuck you, baby."

In disbelief, Thaddeus Bryant also fell down on the sidewalk.

"I'm dying. I'm dying," he said. His voice was small, tinny, and terrified, not like an emperor's at all.

He looked up at Willie Hudson, who had shot him.

"You fucking loser. All of you are losers. Especially you, Brennan."

Terry looked into his eyes. And though the pain in his stomach was near unbearable he managed a small smile.

Thaddeus felt a wave of fury. How could this loser, this mark...how could he...

But he couldn't finish the thought. His eyes rolled back in his head, his charming mouth hung open like a broken drawer, and he died.

CHAPTER THIRTY-SEVEN

Alexander carried a bulging suitcase in one hand and a smaller, tightly packed one in the other. He stood on the corner of 43rd and Third Avenue waiting for a cab to pick him up. It was raining and he had forgotten his umbrella, so water streamed down the back of his neck.

Somehow it was fitting it should rain on his last day in New York.

Though it had been quite a ride working for Nick. Still, all good things must come to an end. He had planned on leaving town after he had found the key to the locker in the 43rd Street bus terminal in Rosalie's apartment. Just about twenty minutes before that pest Terry Brennan had showed up. Ha! The asshole. He'd done his best to convince Nicky that it was Brennan who had stolen the dope, but Nicky hadn't bought it. Who knows who he might be looking at next? Time to split the scene for good.

Now he waited for a cab to come by and he would be out of here. Time to say bye-bye to King Nick. And to Grahame Court, that chamber of horrors.

He was running with the coke and the dough.

And man, he planned on running a long way.

Let it rain. Let it pour. Tomorrow he would be in sunny California.

The day after that, under an assumed name, he would be in his beautiful home in fabulous Tahiti.

Goodbye, New York. If you can make it there, you can make it anywhere...but who the fuck wants to?

He felt the rain come down, shut his eyes for a second and pictured himself on a white beach with clear blue water and native girls surrounding him.

Jesus, the fantasy of every young man, but how many really did it?

He would be among the few.

He opened his eyes and saw a car sitting there in the downpour. It seemed to be waiting for him.

A black limo.

"Oh shit..."

He turned and tried to run, but the slick pavement betrayed him. He fell against a trash can and went sprawling on the street.

When he turned and tried to get up, he saw Bo and Earle standing over him.

"Going somewhere, A?" Bo said.

"Just on a little vacation."

Earle pulled him up, and Bo relieved him of his suitcases.

"Maybe you should let Nick know about your travel plans, motherfucker," Bo said.

"Yeah, man," Earle said. "You being kind of thoughtless. Could hurt the big man's feelings and shit."

Alexander said nothing as they tossed him into the car.

Alexander stood in front of Nicky, who looked down at him from his throne. Next to Alexander were his two bags, as yet unopened.

"You all wet, man," Nick said. "Get our man a fluffy towel, Bo."

Bo disappeared to find the fluffiest towel imaginable.

"So you was going to where?"

"Nicky, I...," Alexander stuttered.

"His ticket say Tahiti," Bo said.

"Ah," Nicky said. "A remarkable place. I once stayed there for two weeks. It was like a dream."

"Nick, let me explain," Alexander said.

Nicky nodded to Earle who slugged Alexander in the right kidney. Alexander groaned as he sagged to the floor.

Nicky nodded and went on with his little talk.

"I been thinking a lot. You realize thinking is what is gonna get black people ahead. Not playing hoops."

Alexander managed a nod.

"And thinking has made me start to wonder. Wonder is what comes from thinking real hard."

"Absolutely right," Alexander said, coughing.

"And I come up with some answers, man. I know who stole the money and the cocaine."

"Really?"

"Yep. 'Course, I know it was Joey. That was obvious. But, thing is, I know who else was a player, too."

"Well, who did you come up with?"

Not the cleverest of comebacks.

Better answer that himself.

"You mean Joey Gardello and Thaddeus Bryant took the dope, right?"

"I do not. I mean Joey Gardello and somebody inside the company took the dope. Somebody who could tell them exactly when the truck was coming off the boat and which route the truck was gonna take to the Manhattan warehouse."

"Yeah, well them two cops mighta done that," Alexander said. His voice cracked a little when he said it.

"Oh yeah, those cops were in on it, yes, sir. Lazenby and Green ran security for the thieves. But they needed a guy inside. Someone to give them our schedule, and I decided, in my time in the garden of thought and wonder, that it was you, A. You are the very fucking one."

"What?" Alexander said. "You accusing me?"

"Yes, afraid I am."

"Who told you that? Who said it? Whoever it was is a bullshitter. Don't be fooled by no bullshitters, Nick. C'mon now."

"I wouldn't be," Nicky said. "Trust me. I am never fooled by bullshitters. My guess is you were going to split with Joey and his pals. But since he was dead, you figured to take it all yourself. Fun in the sun in Tahiti with Paul Gaugin and his native girls."

"No," Alexander said. "No, no, no. I been set up, I tell you. No, man. No."

"Really? Then you won't mind opening them suitcases."

Alexander fell down on his knees and clasped his hands like he was in full prayer mode.

"Christ, Nicky. Give me a break. I didn't know what I was doing. I made a mistake, man."

Nick nodded to Earle to open the suitcases. The big man came over and held out his hand to Alexander, who gave him the key.

Earle twisted the key in the lock and the case sprung open. There, inside, were many packets of bills.

He opened the second case and there were many packets of lovely white powder.

"Where are your clothes, A?" Nicky said. "Guess you were going to buy some new outfits in the islands."

Alexander crawled up to Nicky's Bally shoes.

"Please, please. Them cops made me do it. They had me on a dope bust. They said they would invest it and we'd make so much money that someday I could pay you back with interest. Can't you forgive me this once?"

Nicky smiled and patted Alexander's head, like someone patting a naughty pet. A little rough but not without affection.

"Nah, I do not believe I can," Nicky said.

Then Nicky pulled out his .38 revolver, which sat beneath a pillow on a golden table next to his golden throne.

"Forgiveness? That's for Jesus. He probably forgive you when you show up in Heaven, A."

He then shot Alexander two times in the head and smiled as he watched him die.

CHAPTER THIRTY-EIGHT

Two Weeks After Thaddeus' Death

Lazenby and Green sat in their favorite Blarney Stone Bar at 55th and Seventh Avenue, drinking shots and beer and eating corned beef and cabbage. They both sported bandages on their heads. Lazenby's was so big it looked as though he was wearing a white turban.

"Fuck, fuck, fuck," Lazenby said.

"Fucking joke's on us, Maurice," Green said.

"How's that?" Lazenby said. He powered down his third Jack and felt it burn his throat. It was funny, when you were riding high and drank whiskey it burned your throat, sure, but then it was a "good burn." You smiled big and wide like Burt Lancaster and thought of yourself as a colorful scalawag like "The Crimson Pirate." But when you had just lost your meal ticket to Hollywood where you were promised to be technical advisor on all of Thaddeus's upcoming cop pictures, the whiskey burn just felt like a lit match, minus any macho adjectives that made it palatable. It was just a freaking burn, all the way down to your intestines, and an unpleasant one at that.

"Kid had it all going for him and blew it."

"Yeah, the worst."

"Then we lose the coke too," Green said. "'Cause Alexander gets popped."

"You think he's dead?" Maurice said.

"As dead as Hoffa. Probably buried out in Sheepshead Bay."

"Yeah, suppose so," Lazenby said.

"But, hey, Lazy Bee, don't be sad. 'Cause we are men of genius."

"How so, Greenie?"

"Well, let's think of the positive. Any two cops can double-cross people, but it takes men of genius to pull the old triple cross. I mean we worked for Nicky and double crossed him by throwing in with Alexander and Joey but double crossed them by throwing in with Thaddeus and his weird little moll Gina. That takes genius, wouldn't you say?"

"To us, happy rascals till the end."

Lazenby clicked glasses with Green and after they pounded down their booze Green lay a comradely arm around his partner.

"See, the thing is, great and ingenious men such as us can always create new opportunities, which, by the way, is one of the finest advantages of a career in law enforcement. Correct?"

"Indeed," Maurice said. "Law enforcement is an ever-renewable opportunity for the creative entrepreneur."

"That it is, Maurice. That it is."

They got two more shots for the road, waved goodbye to the counterman, Garecki, and zigzagged their way past the bar's other denizens and out into the not-so-busy late afternoon streets. Rain poured down and Lazenby looked up at the ugly sky.

"The Gloomifier," he said, mocking the downpour.

"A coinable phrase, old pal," Green said. "One that shall live throughout all eternity."

They slid behind the wheel of their Crown Vic. Lazenby at the wheel, his man Green riding shotgun.

Lazenby started to cheer up a bit. They still had a lot going for them.

They were true badasses who drove down the crowded, morally twisted streets of their great city. New York City. The only real city!

They were not unlike Butch and Sundance. Heroes of the concrete and steel range.

Lazenby stuck his key into the ignition of the Crown Vic and turned it on.

"The good old Crown Vic," he said to Detective Green. "Our faithful steed."

Green laughed and pounded the dashboard in an affectionate manner.

As the Semtex bomb which had been planted under the driver's seat went off, they felt much better than they had an hour ago. Onward, upward. A fine feeling.

And their very last feeling.

Their bodies exploded into thousands of pieces, their blood splatter was legendary, and the blast blew out the window of the Blarney Stone, hurting no one but seriously wrecking the steam table.

The two bold detectives made the *New York Post* the next morning. Their headline read: "Blarney Blast Kills Two of Manhattan's Finest."

The two heroes were given a ceremony at HQ with closed coffins, and at the funeral there were sincere speeches made by the chief about finding their killers. But since everyone in the precinct knew they were on the take and exactly who they had crossed, there was no investigation.

Homicide Detectives Maurice Lazenby and Lam Green were forgotten faster than last week's cancelled TV show. And, up in Harlem, Nicky drank a final toast to the end of the Joey Gardello affair.

He would have to get more reliable partners from the NYPD next time out. Those two suckers had no loyalty, none at all. What was the world coming to?

CHAPTER THIRTY-NINE

Three Weeks After Thaddeus' Death

Kathy hurried through down the busy fifth floor of the East Side Presbyterian Hospital, down to Terry's room. She carried a copy of Raymond Chandler's *High Window*, though she knew Terry probably wouldn't want to read much of it considering the shape he was in.

He had been uncommonly lucky. The bullet had passed through his pelvis, exiting out of his side without doing terrible damage. Kathy had been stunned to hear that a shot to the pelvis was probably the luckiest place to be hit. She had assumed that a shot to the pelvis would involve the bullet hitting the spinal column, but the surgeon had explained to her that it was actually rare for the bullet to hit the spine. As it was, muscles had been damaged, but, all in all, Terry had been extremely fortunate. His future would involve rehab, but the best bet would be that he recovered from surgery after a few months.

He was still in intense pain, though, and Dr. Larsen had prescribed a morphine drip for a week. Now he was taking Tylenol and codeine.

As Kathy entered his hospital room, she saw Terry sitting up on a raft of pillows. He was watching *Kiss of*

Death, the original version with Richard Widmark.

"Hey," he said, smiling. "This is the greatest movie."

"I know," Kathy said she said. Then she imitated Widmark as Tommy Udo. "Big man," she said, "You're a real big man! You squirt!"

Terry cracked up and pain shot through his ribs.

"Stop. Too funny. It's killing me."

"You deserve it, you bum," she said. But she was smiling when she said it.

She sat on the edge of the bed and took Terry's hand. "I have some news for you."

"What's that?"

"Your lawyer thinks all charges are being dropped against you. On the basis of that tape you made."

Terry turned off the movie as she leaned over and kissed him.

"That's the best news I've heard in a while."

"Yeah," Kathy said. "But I have some more good news for you. Your agent came into the Head. Has he called you yet?"

"No. Tell me."

"Well, he wouldn't tell me exactly which ones, but it looks like a number of publishers want you to write the story of your friendship with Thaddeus. The real story."

Terry shook his head, winced from a little shot of pain in his stomach and then managed a smile.

"Amazing. And just a few weeks back I didn't think I had any material. I suppose I owe Thaddeus a major debt after all."

Kathy sighed and got up from the bed.

"Yeah," she said. "And they can't stop writing about you in the papers. Not to mention the *60 Minutes* interview."

"The whole thing is crazy," Terry said.

Kathy looked down as she spoke.

"I'll bet you'll be more popular than ever at Elaine's."

Terry laughed.

"Yeah, Mick better move aside."

She looked at him and there was sorrow in her gaze.

"I mean it. You're in a whole new league now."

"Cut it out."

Kathy's voice trembled a bit.

"Models, movie stars, they'll be flocking to your door. Look, Terry, I just want you to know that I understand. That was the one thing Thaddeus was right about. You're becoming a superstar now. The movie deal will be next. You and me. We won't be playing in the same league."

Terry laughed out loud.

"Will you stop?"

Tears suddenly welled in Kathy's eyes.

"It's not funny, Terry. I mean it. You've worked hard and you should be free to, you know, reap the benefits."

"Yeah, that's right," Terry said. "I should. I should go to Hollywood and get a major coke habit and then appear on the Johnny Carson Show and date an endless assortment of bimbos. Then end up in a car wreck down in Malibu and go to rehab with rock stars."

He looked at her and stretched out his arms.

She refused to take his hands.

"No, you can't make light of it. You are a star now. What was that thing Thaddeus said about being a 'stone carrier?' Well, that's what I am. You're not. Not anymore. Stone carriers and stars don't mix. You must see that, Terry."

"Cut it out now, Kathy. Listen to me. A writer, if he's

any good, is always a stone carrier. Real writers write about how good people are screwed over by the Thaddeus Bryants of the world. About the working people who get fucked over by the slick boys in the corporate boardrooms and on Madison Avenue. If a writer sucks up to royalty, then he or she is no good to anybody anymore. If I learned anything from this carnival ride with Thaddeus, it was that."

Kathy looked at him in a longing way, but her eyes were still filled with doubt.

"That sounds great, Terry, just like a writer from the 1930s but when they start throwing the big money at you, maybe it'll be a different story?"

Terry thought about it for a second or too, then said: "Maybe you're right. But I have a pretty good idea. Why don't you come with me? That way you can watch my back."

Kathy rubbed her eyes and looked horribly adorable.

"It's no use, Terry. We're breaking up."

"No, we're not," Terry said.

"We are too," Kathy said.

"The hell we are," Terry said. "As soon as I can walk out of here, we're moving in together."

Kathy blinked and looked at Terry suspiciously.

"We're what?" she said.

"Getting married," Terry said. "That is, if you'll have me?"

He put out both his arms toward her again.

This time she kind of eased into them.

"Well?" he said.

"Well what?" Kathy said.

"Well, will you have me?"

She cried a little more, but she was smiling now.

"I'd be a fool to even think about marrying you. You still don't know who you really are yet. And the big boys haven't gotten their hooks into you yet either."

"Ye of little faith," he said. "Okay, then. Give me a year. If I've turned into a giant Hollywood asshole you can kick me out. But if not...we get married."

She smiled at him and shook her head.

"Okay," Kathy said. "I can live with that."

Then she fell on the bed into his arms.

Terry made a horrible groaning sound.

"Jesus, my side," he said. "You're killing me, kiddo."

"Sorry. But if I'm watching over you, it's going to hurt sometimes."

"Oh, is that right?"

"Yeah, it is," she said. "Dead on."

"Dead on, huh. Let me tell you something, Kathy, I took on Thaddeus Bryant and so I can handle the likes..."

"Oh shut up, Brennan," she said, laughing.

"Shut up? You telling me to shut up?"

"That's right, tough guy," she laughed. "Shut up and kiss me."

"Kiss you? Kiss you?" Terry said. "What the hell?"

He pulled her to him. His side was killing him but when her lips met his it didn't seem to matter at all.

A native of Baltimore, **ROBERT WARD** has worked as a novelist, professor, screenwriter, producer, and actor. He is the author of twelve novels. His first effort was the critically acclaimed novel *Shedding Skin*, which won the National Endowment for the Arts award for first novel of exceptional merit.

BOOKS

On the following pages are a few
more great titles from the
Down & Out Books publishing family.

For a complete list of books and to
sign up for our newsletter,
go to DownAndOutBooks.com.

A Dark Homage
Wendy Tyson

Down & Out Books
January 2020
978-1-64396-074-6

What do a sex tape, a venture capital firm, a secret society of women, and a Catholic nun have in common? Murdered author Miriam Cross.

As Delilah Percy Powers and her staff of female detectives—a militant homemaker, an ex-headmistress, and a former stripper—investigate Miriam's death, they discover a dark criminal underworld. The team takes on Miriam's fight for justice, battling wits against a sadistic killer and putting their own lives at risk.

The Lantern Man
Jon Bassoff

Down & Out Books
February 2020
978-1-64396-076-0

Shortly after her brother, Stormy, is convicted of the brutal murder of a classmate, seventeen-year-old Lizzy Greiner is found dead in an abandoned mountain shack, the result of a fire. Next to Lizzy's charred body, investigators find her journal, safely stored inside a fireproof box. Her narrative calls into question everything investigators thought they knew about the murder. It also calls into question Lizzy's sanity.

At once a mystery, a family drama, and a ghost story, *The Lantern Man* is sure to keep you flipping pages deep into the night.

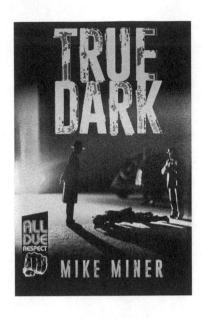

True Dark
Mike Miner

All Due Respect, an imprint of
Down & Out Books
November 2019
978-1-64396-045-6

Set in a tiny border town in eastern California, *True Dark* chronicles the trials and tribulations of the Murphy family.

Mike Miner captures a dangerous world where the lines between good and bad are blurry but the lines between family are black and white.

Coal Black: Stories
Chris McGinley

Shotgun Honey, an imprint of
Down & Out Books
December 2019
978-1-64396-058-6

Set in the hills of eastern Kentucky, these tales lay bare the dark realities of the region. Sometimes the backdrop is the opioid epidemic and all the human detritus and bloodshed that comes with it. Other times it's poachers or petty thieves who take center stage, people whose wild desperation invite danger everywhere they go. High in the hills the action takes place, alongside the rarely seen animals who hunt up there, and sometimes alongside the "haints" and spirits of popular folklore.

Coal Black is a collection of gritty crime stories—cleverly drawn tales with sometimes savage surprise endings.

CPSIA information can be obtained
at www.ICGtesting.com
Printed in the USA
LVHW041653061120
670968LV00005B/861